TROLLEYCARS

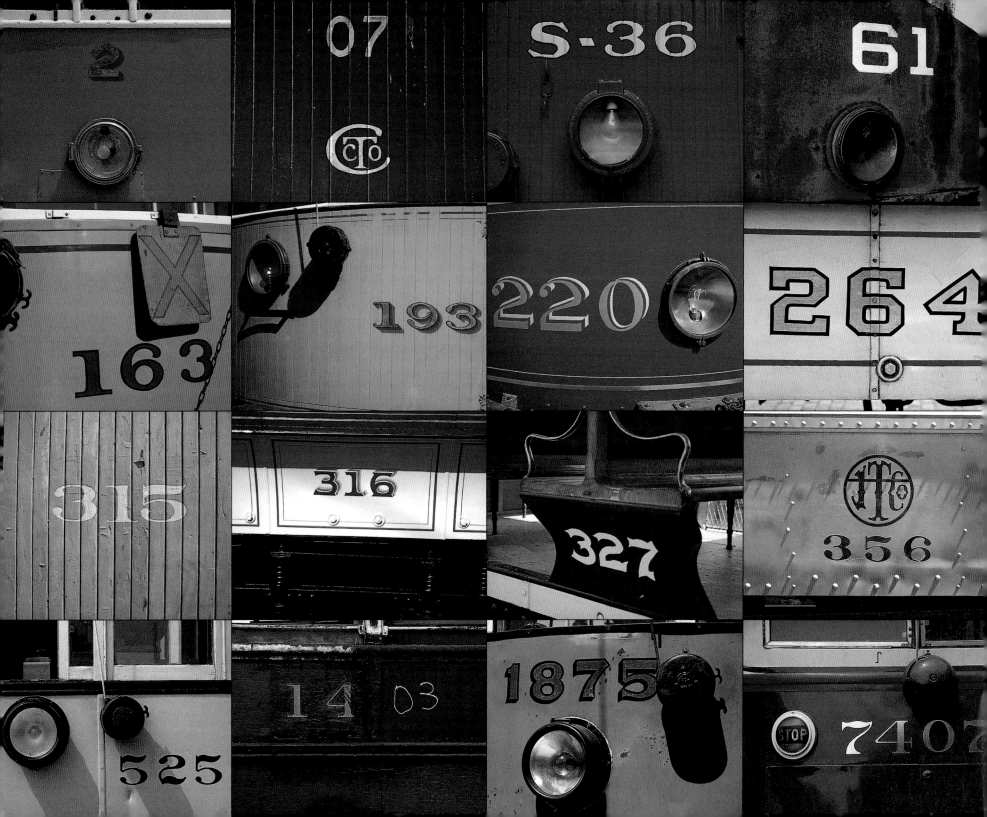

TROLLEYCARS

**STREETCARS, TRAMS AND
TROLLEYS OF NORTH AMERICA:
A PHOTOGRAPHIC HISTORY**

FRANK SULLIVAN AND FRED WINKOWSKI

Motorbooks International
Publishers & Wholesalers ®

DEDICATION
Frank dedicates this book to Iris and to Uncle Art.
Fred dedicates this book to his wife Sally

This edition first published in 1995 by Motorbooks
International Publishers & Wholesalers, PO Box 2,
729 Prospect Avenue, Osceola, WI 54020 USA

Library of Congress Cataloging-in-Publication
Data is Available

ISBN 0-87938-972-9

A QUINTET BOOK

This book was designed and produced by
Quintet Publishing Limited
6 Blundell Street
London N7 9BH

Creative Director: Richard Dewing
Designer: Peter Laws
Managing Editor: Helen Denholm
Editor: Lydia Darbyshire
Photographers: Frank Sullivan and Fred Winkowski

The authors and publishers would like to thank the
following for supplying additional pictures:
National Tramway Museum, Crich
J. H. Price
The London Transport Museum

Typeset in Great Britain by
Central Southern Typesetters, Eastbourne
Manufactured in Singapore by Eray Scan Pte. Ltd.
Printed in Singapore by Star Standard Pte. Ltd.

CONTENTS

INTRODUCTION

Hulks of old trolleys await restoration at Halton County Radial Railway Museum outside Toronto.

If, like the authors, you are over 50 years old, you can probably still remember trolley cars. The cross-breed trolley bus, with its soft tires, which is still numerous in cities like Toronto, Boston and Dayton, doesn't count, and, of course, if you live in a city like San Francisco or Philadelphia, you see trolley cars, maybe even ride them, every day.

Although many European cities have never given them up, for most of us, however, the trolley car disappeared while we were still young. My own memories of these machines are nebulous. I remember yellow, barred windows, sparks and loud snapping noises, and being afraid of the loud, bumpy rides, so unlike the smooth, large-windowed buses we'd take to my grandmother's house. I didn't mind a bit when they were gone, leaving only echoing, abandoned car barns to play in and odd sections of steel track, half-flooded with asphalt.

My co-author remembers a strange type of trolley. He once rode in an excursion car, which had an odd, sloping platform with amphitheater-like seats, for a school trip around Boston, Massachusetts. A friend can even remember the day his mother told him that the trolleys were to run no more and that the buses would start on that very day. Everyone seemed truly excited by this further sign of postwar prosperity and that there would be no more drab, decrepit trolleys!

Now, however, trolley cars awaken our memories of simpler

Thousands of streetcars have gone, but this old center-entry car has been saved and will someday ride the rails again at the Rockhill Trolley Museum.

This PDD awaits restoration to its former glory at the National Capital Trolley Museum.

RIGHT AND
BELOW

To the right is a phone booth in Washington D.C., a view down through the steps of car number 2001 in Connecticut, and a typical trolley pole in Baltimore, Maryland. Below are new trackbeds at the Orange Empire Railway Museum.

times, when the world was in love with the machine, when people commuted to work to the clang of the bell. The gingerbread shapes and colorful liveries are a cheerful relief from the anonymous plastic and glass, smoke-belching buses. And that is one reason why trolleys are due for a serious revival: they are efficient and, at street level, pollution free. It won't be long before trolleys repossess 42nd Street in New York, from which they vanished in 1946. But these trolleys will be lightweight, low-drag bubbles, more in tune with the 21st century than with the trolleys of memory. In fact, they are not even called trolleys any more, but are LRVs, light rail vehicles.

Streetcars are hard to kill. Their carcasses litter the countryside, and although most were burned out and scrapped, some were put to other uses. Even though their weight was prodigious, they were shipped from the U.S. to countries in all parts of the world, and the stalwart, over-engined motors still drive old Brills and PCCs in many cities. Not only are they used as roadside restaurants or cafés, but they have also seen use as a chicken coop and, in Mississippi, even as a church.

ABOVE AND LEFT

The complex web of overhead trolley wires has vanished from most cities, but it has been re-created in the Shore Line Trolley Museum (left) and the Rockhill Trolley Museum (above).

Dedicated groups of enthusiasts in many countries have taken some of the discarded trolleys and streetcars under their care and have carried out the sometimes back-breaking tasks of restoring these machines, often to full running condition. We have sought out some of these collections, and through our photographs we will try to trace the development of these strange, antiquated-looking conveyances. Although some of these cars do not even look like moving vehicles to our modern eyes, each trolley's features were shaped by a logic involving engineering, economics, and public taste.

Strictly speaking, a trolley car is a streetcar that receives its power from overhead power lines by sliding or "trolling" a pole-mounted contact over them. In this book, we are more inclusive; any rolling stock that served on streetcar or inter-urban lines, that is preserved in a museum, and that excites our interest as photographers is a trolley.

CHAPTER ONE

BEFORE THE TROLLEY CAR

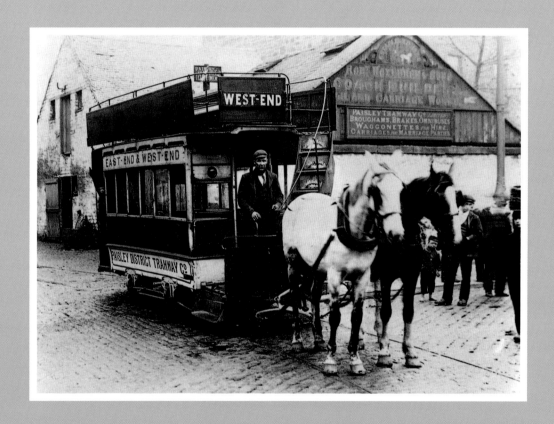

Everyone has a general idea of the history of the steam railroad. It is a dramatic story, with larger than life heroes and villains, and it makes the history of the development of the trolley seem mundane in comparison. At its simplest, a transportation system was needed to replace the system of horse-drawn vehicles that had grown up in cities and outlying towns to transport the growing numbers of workers to and from their jobs. After fruitless experiments with steam, compressed air, naphtha, and even methane gas, the electric trolley was developed to do this menial job. In the process, those city workers gained tremendous freedom to travel unprecedented distances for a nominal fare, to anywhere they might have a yen to go. A ring of suburbs grew up around most cities, and in the U.S. only the greater freedom granted by the automobile could turn people away from the rail-bound trolley.

Before we look at the development of the trolley car, it is worth considering the background of the horse-drawn car, because the trolley car never really lost the look of its animal-powered precursor. The horse car was itself descended from the street omnibus or coach and at first resembled a steel-wheeled stagecoach running on iron straps or tracks that were fastened to wooden strips or stone blocks on the street surface. Later on, tracks were set into the road surface. In the early Stephenson horse cars of the 1830s and 1840s, the driver sat on top, overlooking the team of horses, while the passengers crouched below, handing their fares up through a trap door in the ceiling. Those travelers who were slow to pay could expect to hear the driver's whip rapping sharply on the roof. The horse car's iron wheels were smaller than the spoked, wooden

wheels of the typical carriage, because smooth iron rails had less rolling resistance than the unpaved or cobblestoned streets of the day, but the lower bodies of these first horse cars still had the in-swept curve built into most carriages for wheel clearance. In fact, many early trolley car bodies retained this same "ogee" body section, which allowed wagons and carts to pass by on crowded streets. The cabin above swelled outward to provide hip room.

Later horse cars began to resemble their glamorous steam-powered cousins, and they became, in effect, miniature railroad cars, with straight-sided cabins and clerestory roof designs. The driver descended to a platform in front of the passengers, where he drove the horses or mules from a standing position,

ABOVE
Horse car number 23 belonging to Belfast City Tramways.

and a conductor to collector the fares was added. Wheels shrank to rail car proportions. These design trends were not incompatible, and features were freely mixed. The overriding consideration was that the horse cars should be as light as possible, and their evolution culminated in a combination of the best of the carriage-maker's elegance and the mechanical directness of the rail coach.

With the example of the steam locomotive before them, companies operating horse cars came to realize that draft animals were really not the perfect motive power for urban transportation. They were, after all, living in the industrial age and drawing closer to the unimaginable wonders of the 20th century. A modern city had little use for thousands of manure-producing animals, which could work for only four hours a day and consumed grain by the bushel basket whether they were working or not. That this system was not only archaic but fragile was underscored by a calamity in 1872. In that year began the "great epizootic," a virulent and lethal flu-like disease that killed thousands of horses throughout Canada and the U.S. and halted horsecar service in many cities for weeks. Almost 20,000 horses sickened in New York City alone, and the death rate in Philadelphia approached 200 a day. Desperate cities tried oxen as replacements, and some even used human press gangs to pull the cars, but with little success.

Although the disease seemed to have run its course by 1873, the lesson was plain – find a mechanical substitute for horse power – and so began a decade-long search for a practical powered alternative. Coal-fired steam power, an obvious candidate, was really not appropriate for the large cities,

This early trolley – Union Railways number 316 – has curved side or rocker panels to give clearance for horse-drawn wagons to pass. These early cars had to share the streets with horse-drawn vehicles.

although both New York and London tried the system for a while. The cable car seemed briefly to be the answer. A remote powerplant, which could run an endless loop of cable beneath the street that lightweight cars could grip and thereby haul themselves around, had many advantages and excelled on hills. In 1873 San Francisco, naturally, was the first city to install a practical system, and its cable cars are now a public icon and will probably run forever. Cable cars, although prohibitively expensive, were cheaper than horse cars to maintain, and every city wanted them. Systems were installed in the U.S. in Chicago and Denver, and in Melbourne, Australia, and Wellington, New Zealand, and for a few years the "gripman," as the driver was called, ruled the streets.

His reign was short, however. A buzz of activity produced dozens of competing electric car designs, none of which was wholly practical. William Siemens had some success in Germany. His cars ran sporadically just outside Berlin in 1881, but he used dangerous high-voltage track for power. In the U.S., experimenters such as Daft, who used electric locomotives, and Van Depoele, who pioneered the use of the trolley pole, built lines that were almost profitable. Even Edison played with electric streetcars. Cities such as Frankfurt in Germany, Brussels in Belgium, and Baltimore and Cleveland in the U.S. installed lines – and paid the price of frustrating unreliability. These early systems also created such unforeseen and unwelcome side-effects as hissing and static-ridden telephone lines, electrocuted cats and dogs, and burst water and gas pipes, caused by ground-circuit induced corrosion. Not one of the 10 lines running in 1887 had made any money for the city or its investors.

All the parts of the puzzle were about to be put together by one man, however. In the spring of 1877, the city of Richmond, Virginia, had given a contract to build a 12 mile (19km), 30-car streetcar line to a young ex-Navy officer and engineer, Connecticut-born Frank Sprague. Although he was a successful builder of automobiles, he came fresh from a humiliating failed demonstration of electric car technology to Jay Gould, a potential backer of a New York elevated trolley system. He could easily have failed again, but his naval experience and technical training prepared Sprague for the type of trial and error needed to build a viable system from scratch. His motors, already good by the standards of the times, were combined with a "wheelbarrow" method of mounting to drive wheels that didn't shake them to pieces. He perfected a power regulator and controller that allowed up to 22 cars to start up at once, and, of course, a spring-mounted trolley pole topped the whole ensemble.

Sprague's system worked! Although the line had to scramble to stay functional, it improved almost daily, until even people like Boston horse-car magnate Henry Whitney visited Richmond to investigate. They departed impressed, leaving Sprague with orders. Once Sprague set things in motion, the new system got under way as city after city rolled out their colorful new machines. Soon, cities as distant as Florence in Italy had Sprague trolleys. His company was quickly absorbed by General Electric, and although he stayed on for a while, his name was removed from all patents and even from the trolleys he had worked on, so except for rail and trolley enthusiasts, few know of him today.

In Britain progress was slower, but a network of "trams" was steadily built up, and by 1898 there were 500 cars on 150 miles (240km) of track. The American company Thompson Houston, a successor to Van Depoele, gave the initial impetus to cities like Leeds, while Siemens built a system for the Channel Island of Guernsey. Almost without exception, Britain and parts of the British Empire stuck with double-decker designs for the next 50 years.

European cities might have been expected to evolve dozens of specialized types of streetcar, but, in fact, the opposite happened – each city had its own colorful livery, but underneath they all followed a standard formula. The prototypical European tram was a small, four-wheel, open-platform car, usually running in trains of two or three cars. These narrow-gauge trolleys, directly descended from horse cars, coexisted with small networks of intercity and suburban steam or electric-powered trains, all bearing a strong family resemblance.

A busy scene full of horse cars in the center of Manchester, England.

CHAPTER TWO

THE WHEELS BEGIN TO TURN

THE FIRST TROLLEYS

Our first section traces the outward changes that transformed the horse car-with-motor into the staid urban coach and also into the jaunty excursion car, with body styles ranging from breezy open-siders to cozy, heated Pullmans with plush-covered seats.

The roof-mounted power switch and bell on the Baltimore convertible car.

The elegant iron seats of the open Baltimore traction car.

Once practical trolleys were running in a few cities, local authorities everywhere rushed to install them. As cities electrified and built powerplants, the infrastructure required to switch from horse-drawn cars to trolleys was minimal, for not only could existing track systems be used, but the horse-drawn cars themselves could have motors installed and be up and running on their old routes with minimum delay. This expedient was hardly necessary, however, as new designs poured out of such firms as Stephenson and J. G. Brill. The advances in motor design, which took the early cars from sparking prima donnas to durable, taken-for-granted public utilities, went on behind the scenes, and invisible, except to the technicians and mechanics, were new generations of motors and trucks that could be fitted into existing rolling stock.

Among the early trolleys, there were many different types of design both for interiors and exteriors. They ranged from luxurious heated Pullmans to open-sided cars. Most importantly, weight was no longer a drawback, but actually aided traction, so the bare essential interiors of horse cars, with their wicker or pierced plywood seats, took on a gilded age splendor, and the beautiful steam-bent tulipwood or birchwood sides were duplicated in stamped metal or cast iron.

DERBY LOCO, ENGINE No NUMBER, 1888

SPECIFICATIONS	
LIVERY	DERBY HORSE RAILWAY
TYPE	LOCOMOTIVE
CAR NUMBER	NONE
DATE	1888
BUILDER	PULLMAN
LENGTH	20 FEET (6.1M)
WEIGHT	10,000LB (4,536KG)
SEATS	NONE
TRUCKS/WHEELS	ST

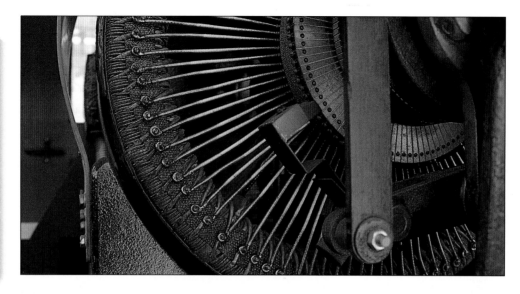

The Derby Electrical Line Motor has the solidity and feel of a tugboat. The motor, which is accessible through center doors, almost fills the interior.

LEFT

The 75-horsepower motor has the over-scale, over-built look of many early prototype electrical mechanisms, but the craftsmanship is apparent.

ABOVE

This complex trolley mechanism could be folded down to pass under bridges or through tunnels.

Can this oddly proportioned, garishly colored device really be a trolley? Strictly speaking, it is an electric locomotive that pulled freight cars, weighing up to 35 tons at a time, but the apparatus at the top is definitely a trolley, and because this is the sole survivor of Connecticut's first trolley line and the world's first electric freight line, dating from 1888, it deserves pride of place in this book. A look at the interior of the Electrical Line Motor shows the huge, centrally mounted motor that delivered 75 horsepower by chain drive to both axles. The wheels were the same as used on railroad cars at the time. Its proportions result from the fact that it could not fit under a low dockside bridge. This led to 2 feet (60cm) being lopped from its cabin height. Its garish colors were those of the Derby Horse Railway.

Although built by Pullman, the motor and equipment were designed by Charles Van Depoele, a pioneer in electric railroad development and the first person to use the spring-mounted overhead trolley to deliver power. In 1887 he had six systems up and running in the U.S. and Canada. When local merchants needed an alternative to the excessive tariffs being charged by the steam railroad, they proposed a short electric line to the Housatonic river's steamers, and, impressed by Van Depoele's newly opened line in Scranton, Pennsylvania, they approached him for the project. This was the last streetcar venture to be completed by Van Depoele before he sold the company to the Thomas Houston Co., which later became part of General Electric. The little car performed well for two years, until the collapse of the steamboat company it served. It was preserved by New Haven Railroad and was eventually purchased by the Branford Museum in 1982.

3RD AVENUE RAILWAY Co., EX-CABLE

NUMBER 220, 1892

LEFT

The ornate graphics showed the pride that owners, passengers, and cities alike felt in possessing such technological marvels.

RIGHT

The curvilinear woodwork is reminiscent of Art Nouveau themes. Bare bulbs, then new, were considered beautiful in themselves. These bulbs are still made in small quantities.

SPECIFICATIONS	
LIVERY	3RD AVENUE RAILWAY CO.
TYPE	CLOSED
CAR NUMBER	220
DATE	1892
BUILDER	LA CLEDE CAR CO.
LENGTH	32 FEET (9.8M)
WEIGHT	23,000LB (10,433KG)
SEATS	20
TRUCKS/WHEELS	ST

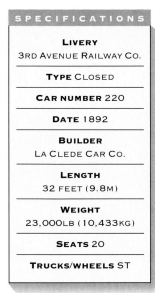

When New York abandoned cable cars for trolleys, the downtown areas refused to use overhead wiring for power and, shrewdly, retained the underground cable ways from the old system. In the 1870s and 1880s, as New York became the center of finance and communication, the telegraph, telephone, and electric power lines strung from wooden poles in the streets grew into dense, overhead webs. The vulnerability of this ad hoc network was obvious, but the great blizzard of 1888, which brought down almost every line in the city, caused these dangerous eyesores to be banished underground. Manhattan trolleys were forced to use a system of underground conduits. Sliding contacts or "plows" under the cars tapped power from the buried "hot" rails running under the center of the tracks. Comparable systems were installed in Washington, D.C., and Paris, France, for esthetic reasons.

Larger lines, such as the 3rd Avenue Railway Co., were able to make use of their old cable runs and even converted their fleets of cable cars to electric power. Number 220 was one of these. Before its conversion in 1899, number 20, as it was then numbered, had seen seven years of cable service. The La Clede Car Co. had built 200 similar cars for the 3rd Avenue Main Line. Over the years, the platform ends were enclosed so it would resemble more modern cars, but by 1908, number 220 was relegated to use as a "slot scraper," removing ice and debris from the conduit slot, for another 40 years until the demise of New York's trolleys in 1948. The Shore Line Trolley

A "bully pulpit" for the driver (above) shows that the controller is not in place, but the gooseneck brake lever stands out. The image below is a bearing detail of the Peckham trucks, which have been in place since 1908.

Museum acquired the car at that time, restoring it completely with the original open platforms. Remnants of the horse-drawn and cable car origins can be seen over these platforms, their separate hoods blending oddly with the brow-ended "ogee" roof above the passenger compartment, but a rare round-ended clerestory canopy somehow helps to unite all these elements. A glance inside shows the breathtaking virtuosity of the woodwork, where the roof-top elements are clad in sinuously worked bird's-eye maple veneer and fitted with elaborate chandeliers.

When car number 220 started operations, large stretches of 3rd Avenue were undeveloped. Here, it is seen near Long Island Sound marshes in Connecticut.

SPECIFICATIONS	
LIVERY	UNION RAILWAY
TYPE	CLOSED WOOD
CAR NUMBER	316
DATE	1895
BUILDER	AMERICAN CAR CO.
LENGTH	30 FEET (9.1M)
WEIGHT	17,000LB (7,711KG)
SEATS	20
TRUCKS/WHEELS	ST

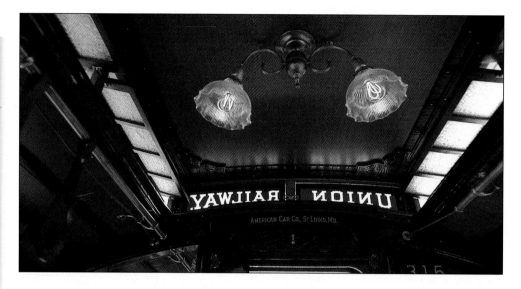

OPPOSITE

There were many "Union Railways" through the northern U.S. in the 1890s. Even after 30 years, the Civil War still remained in people's memories.

LEFT

The oak veneer ceiling was hard to replicate. The ruby glass route sign glowed at night.

One of the earliest cars preserved anywhere, car number 316 is a centerpiece of the Shore Line Trolley Museum's collection. All the handsome regalia of *fin-de-siècle* trolley travel are incorporated in this Union Railway car, dating from 1895, which ran through Bronx and Westchester counties in New York. Still only slightly larger than horse-car size, but weighing several tons more, it was built before the trend to larger double truck or eight-wheeled cars. Single truck designs were preferred in the generally narrower and more winding streets of the cities of Europe, as they were on continental railroads as well.

In spite of the bumpy ride of the single truck New York car, most of the passengers' creature comforts were catered for. Plush seats, bronze fittings, quarter-sawn oak veneer with mahogany trim, and large plate glass windows combine to suggest genteel luxury. The etched glass in the clerestory windows not only looked sophisticated, but also served to denote the route, as did the red and cream paintwork. A similar livery was worn by the later 3rd Avenue Railway Co., which took over Union's routes.

In some ways, the story of the restoration of number 316 is more intriguing than that of her service years, which ended after a stint as a barred-window pay car. Three generations of the Infante family have worked on this car, which was acquired for the princely sum of $350 in 1947. The slow restoration was halted in the 1960s, resumed in the 1990s, and has finally been completed. The windshield over the dashboard, undoubtedly a later addition, has been left *in situ*, but otherwise number 316 is much as it looked when it was rolled out by the American Car Co. in 1895.

KYOTO, CLOSED TRAM NUMBER 19, 1898

SPECIFICATIONS

LIVERY	KYOTO
TYPE	CLOSED
CAR NUMBER	19
DATE	1898
BUILDER	NOT KNOWN
LENGTH	27FT. 8IN. (8.5M)
WEIGHT	18,200LB (8,225KG)
SEATS	40
TRUCKS/WHEELS	ST

BELOW

There is a curious London-built Shorts controller in the cab of number 19.

ABOVE

Although this photograph was taken in California, number 19's pagoda-like clerestory is reminiscent of the temple city of Kyoto.

RIGHT

The interior of the car, with its natural hues and simple materials, is strongly evocative of Japan.

Looking rather somber in the California sunshine, car number 19 is little changed from the day it was decommissioned in 1961 – even the Japanese advertising cards are still in place. From the exterior, however, there is little of Japan about this car, except the restrained markings. This is only natural because number 19 is a U.S. car, which was shipped in kit form for assembly in Kyoto around 1898. This city had Japan's first electric trolley network, a narrow-gauge system. The car is typical of the period, with its double-ended body and single trucks. The wooden body, deck roof, and austere paint scheme undoubtedly helped it blend into the environs of Kyoto, an ancient city of sacred temples. Later Japanese trolley lines also continued to exhibit some U.S. influence, usually having larger double-truck cars. There are no more streetcars in Kyoto. The system has been replaced by a subway, so there is little to mar the beauty of the city.

CONNECTICUT, DOUBLE TRUCK WOOD

Exhibiting the typical tapered end roof caps and the straight-sided wood paneling of the steam railroad Pullman cars is Connecticut Car Co. number 193, which dates from 1904. The heavy bogie, or double-truck, cars of the typical city trolley had begun to appear, but the ornate paintwork and interior mahogany woodwork still show signs of its smaller fore-runners. Number 193 worked the streets of downtown New Haven until 1948, despite the fact that it had been designed for suburban use. Although the totally enclosed design was relatively weatherproof, the tiny doors and huge steps made boarding difficult.

RIGHT

The heavy Pullman roof is very visible in this view and gives number 193 a more purposeful look than the coach – a bit like the four-wheelers just 5 years previously.

ABOVE AND BELOW

Look closely at the lacquered veneer ceiling (above) – Paris green with gold striping. The driver's instruments (below) date from 1904; the air brake gauge is a later addition.

If there is a quintessential trolley experience, it must be a ride in an open car. From the days of the horse car up until the present, whether you are in Lisbon, Portugal, or San Jose, California, the best trolley ride is open to the breezes. In the early days of the trolley, there was not much difference between closed and open cars, because the platforms at front and rear had little more than a waist-high dashboard on both types of cars. Nevertheless, when summer came, the public wanted open cars, and even in Canada and the north of England, the closed cars would be put in the sheds and out would come the "breezers." Of all the open cars, none was more open than the "toast-rack" cars that many British coastal resorts rolled out each summer. Little more than platforms on wheels, with transverse bench seats and step rails along the sides, they could be found at Southport and Blackpool and Llandudno, Wales, where they ran until the 1950s.

Many car companies possessed two fleets of trolleys, one open and one closed. The transit lines hated the expense and inefficiency of this, but they were partly to blame. To increase passenger revenue, they had encouraged people to take weekend and vacation excursion tours and special trips. How many people at the turn of the century had any other way to feel the cooling rush of air as they spun through meadows and woods at a galloping 15mph (24kph) on a hot July day? Companies financed and built parks at the ends of their lines to encourage traffic, fanciful places with picnic grounds, bandstands, dance halls, games fields, "scenic railways" or roller coasters, all magically lit and powered with electricity from the same sources as the trolleys themselves. There was Luna Park, Washington; Overlook Park, Ohio, with its automatic piano; Willow Grove Park's Electric Fountain; and countless others. Ravinia Park,

Illinois, even had the Chicago Symphony Orchestra. Despite this, the companies hated the open cars, although they loved the revenue they brought in. The open benches and full-length step rails encouraged people to leap on and off cars while they were in motion, so increasing accident rates. Perhaps worst of all from the company's view, passengers were able to avoid the conductor and "beat the fare." As new, harder-to-beat fare collection plans evolved in the closed cars, the open cars disappeared from all but the hardiest tourist lines. A few of these lines still run, allowing us to journey from one century's end to an earlier, simpler one, when folks could sing: *"Let's take a ride to the ocean side, where the shining lights are grand."*

ABOVE

Toronto open car number 327 seen cruising short straight-away to the East Loop at the Halton County Radial Railway Museum.

THE WHEELS BEGIN TO TURN

TORONTO, OPEN NUMBER 327, 1893

SPECIFICATIONS

LIVERY	TORONTO TRANSIT
TYPE	OPEN
CAR NUMBER	327
DATE	1893
BUILDER	TORONTO RAILWAY CO.
LENGTH	27½ FEET (8.1M)
WEIGHT	20,000LB (9,072KG)
SEATS	50
TRUCKS/WHEELS	ST

RIGHT

The prominent metal screen on the street side was designed to stop people from exiting into traffic; it is not original.

Although "Old 327" is an authentic evocation of the early days of the trolley, it is really a replica built in 1934, Toronto's centennial year. The Toronto Railway Co. originally ran these cars from 1893 on its downtown routes but stopped in 1915. The two-step, full-length side running boards, although convenient for the long-skirted dresses of women passengers, made them too dangerous for street use at a time when the number of automobiles was increasing.

Open cars like this could be used only during Toronto's short summers, and a thunderstorm would put the motorman in great danger from the nearly 600 volts, only a wooden handle away from his hand.

The original plans were used for the reconstruction of the four-wheeler, and attention has been lavished on the brass armrests, the alternating shades of wood on the seat slats, and the elegant paintwork. The roof-end "brow" houses colored lights for signaling the route to passengers at night. Even the trucks powering the car are antiques, having been made in Montreal before 1900, and they are doubly rare because no other Canadian running gear of the type survives.

ABOVE

The wooden-handled controller regulates the supply of 600 volts power to two wheel-mounted motors.

BALTIMORE TRACTION, OPEN NUMBER 544, 1896

The graceful seat backs flip over to change direction on this double-ended car.

Many designs of "pilots," or cow catchers, were developed to tackle the problem of stopping people from falling under the wheels. This one looks as inviting as a summer hammock.

SPECIFICATIONS

LIVERY	BALTIMORE TRACTION CO.
TYPE	OPEN
CAR NUMBER	554
DATE	1896
BUILDER	BROWNELL
LENGTH	31 FEET (9.4M)
WEIGHT	17,850LB (8,097KG)
SEATS	45
TRUCKS/WHEELS	ST

Still redolent of the era of the horse car, one of Baltimore's oldest cars retains the short wheelbase, single-truck construction, but has grown in size and weight to seat 45 people on its lathe-turned wooden benches. Because the seats ran crosswise, the conductor and passengers were forced to clamber onto the full-length running boards on either side of the car. It took a keen-eyed, limber conductor to make sure everyone paid.

By 1919 even the public's love affair with open cars could not keep the old cars running. The mechanical brakes and side running boards were just too dangerous. Number 554's later career, like that of many other older cars, was as an ice scraper numbered work car 3390. The first digit of the original number 554 indicated the route line – in this case, the Huntington Avenue line in Baltimore, the car's first assignment.

The mechanical details are crude but efficient, and will last forever, like this gooseneck brake lever.

Could anything be more evocative of summer than an open trolley car? Note the short wheelbase, single-truck design.

CONNECTICUT CAR COMPANY, OPEN NUMBER 1414, 1911

SPECIFICATIONS

LIVERY	CONNECTICUT CAR CO.
TYPE	OPEN
CAR NUMBER	1414
DATE	1911
BUILDER	OSGOOD BRADLEY
LENGTH	41 FEET (12.5M)
WEIGHT	41,500LB (18,825KG)
SEATS	75
TRUCKS/WHEELS	DT

All aboard for the Yale Bowl! Every October, as the college football season opened and the Yale eleven did battle, number 1414 and 100 superannuated stablemates were wheeled out of the New Haven, Connecticut, sheds to carry the weekend crowds. People outdid each other in crowding onto the open cars, finding any available toehold and scrambling onto the roof until the cars resembled something that might be seen in India or Mexico rather than in a staid university city. So it was that this fall ritual ensured the survival of open cars like number 1414 until a few years past World War II, long after its contemporaries had disappeared.

ABOVE

These open cars had all the ebullient good cheer of a circus car.

RIGHT

The 15 bench seats and double running boards provided plenty of room for football fans to perch on during runs to the Yale Bowl.

OPPOSITE

One of the last open cars to be built in the U.S., number 1414 served in Connecticut, where it runs to this day at the Branford Museum.

UNITED RAILWAYS, OPEN NUMBER 1164, 1902

LIVERY	UNITED RAILWAY & ELECTRIC CO.
TYPE	OPEN
CAR NUMBER	1164
DATE	1902
BUILDER	J.G. BRILL
LENGTH	40½ FEET (12.3M)
WEIGHT	30,740LB (13,944KG)
SEATS	60
TRUCKS/WHEELS	DT

For anyone in sweltering Baltimore on a summer weekend in 1905, the name Riverview Park would conjure up images of water-borne breezes in faraway Tortuga or the Windward Isles. But for a nickel and a few minutes' ride on a car like this, people could travel to their own little paradise, just outside town. The flickering, clear glass bulbs cast a firefly glow through the colored glass of the clerestory windows, as the brass band, in candystriped jackets and straw boaters, pumped out the Sousa marches. The park has gone now, and only this car remains of a flotilla of 110 that for 20 years brought the citizens of Baltimore relief from the airless southern summer.

The United Railway & Electric Co. thought it the height of efficiency to buy one set of trucks and wheels and two sets of bodies for its new fleet in 1902. Thus 110 enclosed bodies sat idle in mild weather, but were exchanged each fall for the airy, awning-bedecked open cars.

BELOW

The driver's platform on number 1164 has the spare functionality of the bridge of a sailing ship.

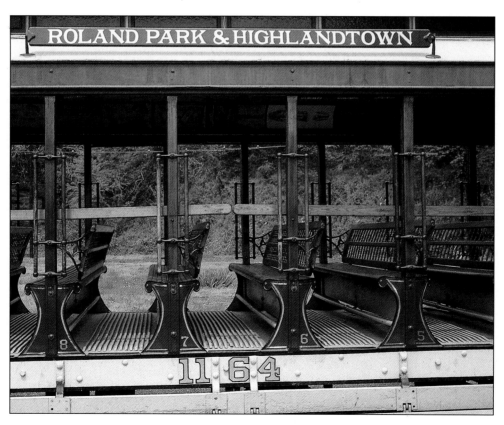

OPPOSITE

Baltimore Streetcar Museum which houses number 1164 is located in downtown Baltimore, Maryland, and its cars run near to the same routes they pioneered 90 years ago.

LEFT

Permanently affixed to the car, the "letter board" gave basic route or company names.

RIO DE JANEIRO, OPEN NUMBER 1875, 1912

SPECIFICATIONS

LIVERY	RIO DE JANEIRO
TYPE	OPEN
CAR NUMBER	1875
DATE	1912
BUILDER	CIA DE TRANSPORTES COLECTIVOS
LENGTH	40 FEET (12.2M)
WEIGHT	40,000LB (18,144KG) EST.
SEATS	65
TRUCKS/WHEELS	DT

When they began constructing trolley systems, most South American countries looked to the U.S. model. A case in point is this open car, which was built by the Cia de Transportes Colectivos de Estado da Guanabara for its service in Rio de Janeiro. A J. G. Brill design from the U.S. was used, but the wood came from Brazilian forests. It is believed that trucks and other metal fittings came from the St. Louis Car Co. Perfectly suited for Rio's weather, this type of car continued to run until the mid-1960s. Unfortunately, it now wears a spurious, if attractive, color scheme and the insignia of Railways to Yesterday, Inc., of the Rockhill Trolley Museum in Pennsylvania.

ABOVE

Curvaceous seats, bright jungle colors, and jutting grab rails put one in mind of a merry-go-round.

RIGHT

Gliding through backwoods Pennsylvania in number 1875 makes a pleasant jaunt on a warm spring day.

BLACKPOOL, OPEN NUMBER 166, 1927

33

SPECIFICATIONS

LIVERY	BLACKPOOL
TYPE	OPEN
CAR NUMBER	166
DATE	1927
BUILDER	BLACKPOOL CORPORATION TRANSPORT
LENGTH	38 FEET (11.6M)
WEIGHT	NOT KNOWN
SEATS	64
TRUCKS/WHEELS	DT

This is about as minimal as a trolley car can get, but for good weather in a resort area such as Blackpool, England, it is all that is needed. Although most of the original Blackpool "toast racks" were built before World War I, this larger, double truck, 64-seater entered service in 1927. The maypole-like trolley pole support was festooned with lights when the tram partici-

pated in the Blackpool Illuminations, when the whole of Blackpool seafront was decorated with lights. In 1953, number 166 was converted into a television platform car to cover the parade that accompanied the Illuminations, and so it was saved for preservation. It is now at the National Tramway Museum at Crich in its restored red livery and lights.

RIGHT

Number 166 trundles down Tramway Street at the National Tramway Museum on a perfect sunny day, where antique cars and buses help to re-create the era of the open tram.

The Orange Empire Railway Museum evokes perfectly the small-town flavor that much of Los Angeles had when cars like this California car owned the streets.

As much as the public loved open cars, the trolley companies resisted demands to provide two sets of cars for good and bad weather, or even to have two sets of bodies, as was tried in Baltimore and a few other places. Several designs attempted to combine the best of both, and these were the convertible cars. Most of these cars originated in Canada and the U.S., because after the demise of the horse-drawn car, most European models were closed-bodied cars, except for the driver's platform, which remained open until the 1920s, much later than on U.S. trolleys.

In Britain, the word convertible referred primarily to the upper deck of double-decker trams, the lower parts of which were almost always closed. Of these "convertibles," the Kensington cover, which was used in Hull and which had roll-top-desk-type panels that slid over covered-wagon-type arched ribs, and the Bellamy-roofed Liverpool trams, which used removable flat panels of similar design, were the most notable.

Some of the earliest attempts to obviate the need to have two fleets of cars were the half-and-half designs, known as "California" cars, such as those still in use on San Francisco's cable cars. The flaw in the design is that on sunny days everyone wants to be outside, but when it rains, people huddle inside, so half the car's capacity is always unused.

As with many of the innovations in trolley design, the true convertible seems to have begun in Canada. In Toronto in 1904, cars were designed with removable side panels, which could be changed in the sheds. Some single-ended cars were built as "near-side convertibles," with only one side (the one away from traffic) removable. Others were more flexible and could be changed quickly, "in case of a change in the weather." Brill had one with straight-sided panels that slid up into the roof. There was also the Duplex design, which used curved sliding panels; these last were known as semi-convertibles.

Open cars and convertibles both died out during World War I, and for the same reasons. The dangers of boarding open cars, especially as traffic on the streets and the transportation companies' preoccupation with fare dodging increased, meant that only a few tourist-type open or convertible cars survived into the 1920s and 1930s. One exception, surprisingly, was in New York, where the convertible cars remained in day-to-day service throughout Brooklyn until after World War II. Perhaps the secret of their longevity was the open metal grillework that replaced the windows in summer and kept passengers from losing the odd arm or leg in the brutal New York traffic.

BALTIMORE CONVERTIBLE NUMBER 264, 1900

SPECIFICATIONS

LIVERY
BALTIMORE TRACTION CO.

TYPE CONVERTIBLE

CAR NUMBER 264

DATE 1900

BUILDER BROWNELL

LENGTH
39½ FEET (12.1M)

WEIGHT
31,700LB (14,409KG)

SEATS 46

TRUCKS/WHEELS DT

ABOVE

A close-up of number 264's (a) brake lever polished by 95 years hard use.

LEFT

Car number 264 is seen returning to the sheds in the golden afternoon sunlight of a long spring day.

ABOVE

Elegant materials were simply used. The central portion of the chandelier is a kerosene lamp for use when power failed.

As a convertible, number 264 may have been a compromise in some respects, but there was certainly no compromise in regard to craftsmanship and quality of woodwork. Beautiful restoration work by the Baltimore Streetcar Museum has revealed the brow-mounted glass "Carey Street" route sign, ornate chandeliers, solid hardwood interiors, and brass fittings.

In cold weather all would be enclosed by tall glass window panels, kept in sheds in summer. The platforms remain open, except for a "portable vestibule," with windows for the driver.

The arrival of longer cars – number 264 is nearly 40 feet (12.1m) – made double-truck wheels or bogies a necessity. "Maximum traction" trucks were a transition type, with only one motor to each truck being, again, a compromise. The smaller, or follower, wheel steered the truck around curves, while the larger wheel, which was powered, took most of the weight of the car. Two motors were cheaper than four to run, but such heavy loads really needed to be spread out over eight wheels, so the use of maximum traction trucks caused maintenance headaches as bearings and wheels wore out.

OPORTO DOUBLE TRUCK NUMBER 249, 1904

Southern Portugal may be the largest trolley museum in the world. Lisbon still runs a miscellaneous collection of U.S.- and Portuguese-built Brill-designed cars from the 1910s, together with some open cars, a funicular, and an assortment of British double-decker trolley buses. Sintra, a resort town not far from Lisbon, runs a 1903 J. G. Brill open car down to the beach in summer. Oporto, Portugal's second-largest city also runs three lines with old, arch-roofed Brills and other cars, although not in the town center anymore. One survivor from

Oporto has resurfaced at the Rockhill Museum in Pennsylvania. Brill built this semi-convertible car in 1904, using standard-gauge maximum traction trucks, although the car itself is quite narrow. It has been modified for one-man operation. When number 249 was taken out of service in 1972, Oporto trolleys were not festooned with "super graphic" advertisements as they are today. However, the Servico de Transportes Colectivos do Porto crest and the "Boavista" destination stencil certainly have the feel of the genuine article.

Although it has 90 years on the clock, number 249 still puts in a full day with the tourists at the Rockhill Trolley Museum.

The original back-lit stencil route signs on number 249 are primitive but attractive.

SPECIFICATIONS	
LIVERY SERVICO DE TRANSPORTES COLECTIVOS DO PORTO	
TYPE SEMI-CONVERTIBLE	
CAR NUMBER 249	
DATE 1904	
BUILDER J.G. BRILL	
LENGTH 35FT. 4IN. (10.8M)	
WEIGHT 30,000LB (13,636KG) EST.	
SEATS 32	
TRUCKS/WHEELS DT	

Once inside the narrow but comfortable car (left), it is easy to imagine you are on the sunny Portuguese coast. Years of continuous manhandling have given this brake wheel (right) the patina of antique bronze.

LOS ANGELES RAILWAY, CALIFORNIA CAR

NUMBERS 525 AND 665, 1905 AND 1911

SPECIFICATIONS

LIVERY
LOS ANGELES RAILWAY

TYPE CALIFORNIA

CAR NUMBER 525

DATE 1905

BUILDER ST. LOUIS
CAR CO.

LENGTH
44FT. 7IN. (13.6M)

WEIGHT
43,000LB. (19,505KG)

SEATS 44

TRUCKS/WHEELS DT

SPECIFICATIONS

LIVERY
LOS ANGELES RAILWAY

TYPE CALIFORNIA

CAR NUMBER 665

DATE 1911

BUILDER
ST. LOUIS CAR CO.

LENGTH
44FT. 7IN. (13.6M)

WEIGHT
37,500LB. (17,010KG)

SEATS 48

TRUCKS/WHEELS DT

LEFT

The interior of a California car is the essence of openness and light. Although the comfort of the seats left much to be desired, durability was the prime consideration.

RIGHT

A close-up of trolley pole swivel and spring.

OPPOSITE

Trundling down a dusty California street, these unflappable cars once played straight man to peripatetic tin lizzies scuttling around them in countless silent movies.

Two typical Huntington standard-type cars from 1905 and 1911 show off the distinctive curved glass windshield side panels that they and 750 similar cars sported on the Los Angeles Railway. The freestanding "jeweled" route letter panels are also notable. These wooden-bodied California-style cars were reputedly designed by H. E. Huntington himself, and they were built by the St. Louis Car Co. Look out for them in various Keystone Cops and Laurel and Hardy movies – and, of course, at the Orange Empire Railway Museum in Perris, California, where they have been restored to running condition.

LEFT AND ABOVE

A headlight detail from number 525 (left). Although they are slightly different shades of yellow, all were city cars (above); red was used for the interurban "Big Red" cars.

BROOKLYN RAPID TRANSIT COMPANY, CONVERTIBLE

NUMBER 4573, 1906

SPECIFICATIONS	
LIVERY	BROOKLYN RAPID TRANSIT CO.
TYPE	CONVERTIBLE
CAR NUMBER	4573
DATE	1906
BUILDER	LACONIA CO.
LENGTH	43 FEET (13.1M)
WEIGHT	48,500LB. (22,000KG)
SEATS	44
TRUCKS/WHEELS	DT

One of the convertible cars that ran very successfully for so many years in New York was number 4573, which was used by the Brooklyn Rapid Transit Co. Although true open cars disappeared from Brooklyn in 1932, these convertibles remained in use until 1947. They were the last of their kind in regular service. Made to an elegant 1906 design by the little known Laconia Co., these cars had large three-quarter length glass panels running down the sides, which were removed in milder months and replaced by horizontal metal grilles. A continuous open space then extended from ceiling to almost floor level, giving all the advantages of a breezy open car, but having in addition the center aisle and restricted entry of the closed car. The 3rd Avenue Railway Co. also ran similar J. G. Brill-built convertibles.

LOS ANGELES RAILWAY, CALIFORNIA CAR
NUMBER 1201, 1921

<table>
<tr><td colspan="2">SPECIFICATIONS</td></tr>
<tr><td>LIVERY</td><td>LOS ANGELES RAILWAY</td></tr>
<tr><td>TYPE</td><td>CALIFORNIA</td></tr>
<tr><td>CAR NUMBER</td><td>1201</td></tr>
<tr><td>DATE</td><td>1921</td></tr>
<tr><td>BUILDER</td><td>ST. LOUIS CAR CO.</td></tr>
<tr><td>LENGTH</td><td>48 FEET (14.6M)</td></tr>
<tr><td>WEIGHT</td><td>44,500LB. (20,185KG)</td></tr>
<tr><td>SEATS</td><td>48</td></tr>
<tr><td>TRUCKS/WHEELS</td><td>DT</td></tr>
</table>

One of the later Los Angeles standard trolleys, number 1201 is really a California-type car, although you have to look closely. Only the six center windows on each side have glass panes; the rest are permanently open, continuing a tradition of 40 years standing. The climate of Los Angeles allowed these cars to come into their own, and on most days, only the smog could force passengers into the closed cabin.

Los Angeles cars ran on narrow-gauge track, only 3½ feet (1.1m) wide, but this 1921 St. Louis Car Co. car was no lightweight – It weighs 2¼ tons and has 48 seats.

RIGHT

Before air conditioning, California cars like number 1201 provided a breath of fresh air amid the haze and palms of greater Los Angeles.

ABOVE

Strongly and heavily built of steel, number 1201 carries the yellow and black livery of the Los Angeles Railway, which later became Los Angeles Transit. Apart from the car number, there is no identification.

Adding a second tier to a trolley to increase its capacity would seem a logical idea. Weight is not a problem, the speeds are low, and, except where bridges or tunnels might dictate height, the sky seems to be the limit. Only in Britain, however, were double-deckers the norm. In the rest of Europe, only one city, Copenhagen, used double-deckers exclusively, in a small system at the turn of the century.

They were not used in the U.S. either, after a few disastrous experiments, notably the infamous "Broadway Battleship," which lumbered around New York for a few years before World War I. The "Battleship" had problems because of the claustrophobia and intolerable crowding induced by its odd one-and-a-half deck layout. Double-deckers were also used briefly in Pittsburgh with similarly bad results. A few were used in places like Coronado Beach, California, where the open air delights of the upper deck outweighed any frustrating delays caused by getting passengers up and down the stairs.

In Britain, any trolley worthy of the name was a double-decker. Many early British horse cars had lightly built, uncovered second tiers above; and as electrification got underway, double-decked, single truck cars prevailed, as did the perverse obsession (given the typical weather) with open cars. In the south-west of England, where the weather was slightly better, not one trolley with a roof was ever operated, except for a few single-deckers. Throughout the greater part of the British Isles, both decks were gradually enclosed. The trend started with the lower deck and extended up and out, with first fabric, then solid panels being used, until totally shut-in, turtle-like cars appeared, a style epitomized by the Glasgow "Cunarders" of the 1950s.

ABOVE LEFT AND RIGHT

A spiral stair to the upper deck of the Dublin double-decker, where there is a bare minimum of upper deck seating, which is typical of most open double-decker trolleys in England.

DUBLIN, DOUBLE-DECKER NUMBER 2, 1901

HOWTH—HILL OF HOWTH— SUTTON

SPECIFICATIONS

LIVERY
GREAT NORTHERN
RAILWAY, IRELAND

TYPE DOUBLE-DECKER

CAR NUMBER 2

DATE 1901

BUILDER BRUSH CO.

LENGTH
30 FEET (9.1 M)

WEIGHT
30,000 LB. (13,608 KG)

SEATS 67

TRUCKS/WHEELS DT

This Dublin trolley is an early step in the evolution of the double-decker trams. Cars like these dating from 1901, were actually operated by the Great Northern Railway until its dissolution in 1958, and for a year after by the CIE, the Coras lompair Eirann, or Ireland's Transport System. Pastoral and scenic, the Hill of Howth Tramway just outside Dublin could be best appreciated from the completely open upper deck of cars like number 2. Two million miles after its construction by the UK Brush Co., number 2 was shipped to the Orange Empire Railway Museum in California for a complete restoration. Another Hill of Howth car, number 10, went to the National Tramway Museum at Crich in England. That trolley has an unusual, naturally finished mahogany exterior livery, but number 2 is finished in the colors of the Great Northern

ABOVE LEFT AND RIGHT

Although it looks a bit out of place in the middle of the California desert, the Great Northern Railway's number 2 has been given a new lease of life *at the Orange Empire Railway Museum.*

Railway. The enclosed platforms were probably added at a later date. A mahogany finished ribbed ceiling and original brass fittings give this Dublin car a nautical feel. The bogie trucks are notable, but there is only one motor per truck.

By the early 1930s, most of the trolleys running in the city of Dublin were built to be fully enclosed on both decks, but even then, Dublin had started to abandon its trolley lines, with the last running, except for these survivors, in 1949.

LEFT AND ABOVE RIGHT AND LEFT

Inside, the look of a ship of the line continues with brass door fittings (left) and bulkhead details and signs (above right). Mahogany ribbing on the ceiling (above), some restored, some new.

LEFT

The sagging old hull in this view recalls a man o' war, needing just a few cannons poking from its "gunwales."

SPECIFICATIONS

LIVERY
GLASGOW, SCOTLAND

TYPE DOUBLE-DECKER

CAR NUMBER 22

DATE 1922

BUILDER GLASGOW CORPORATION TRAMWAYS

LENGTH
30 FEET (9.1M)

WEIGHT
21,280LB. (9,673KG)

SEATS 62

TRUCKS/WHEELS ST

Glasgow's colorful trams underwent continuous modification and modernization throughout their long lives. Car number 22, which was built in 1922, originally appeared as it is today – with closed platforms and upper deck, but with open-roofed balconies, one of the last of the type to appear in Glasgow. Later, the deck was completely closed, and the trolley was kept up to date mechanically until being withdrawn from service in 1960.

The National Tramway Museum has rebuilt it and restored the original Glasgow color scheme. An orange lower band was constant, while the upper band could be red, green, blue, yellow, or white (as shown here), and the dark maroon trim adds contrast to a highly visible livery that dates from the 1890s. Yellow, black, and silver stripes make for a royal coach indeed, which is fitting; Britain's Prince Philip and Prince Charles rode in number 22 at the Glasgow Garden Festival in 1988.

RIGHT

There are many antique features on Glasgow number 22, such as the curved rocker panels, filigree brackets on the roof, and colored glass transom windows. It looks more than 10 years older than Leeds number 180 behind it, which was built in 1931.

LEEDS, DOUBLE-DECKER
NUMBER 399, 1925

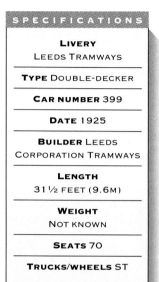

SPECIFICATIONS	
LIVERY	LEEDS TRAMWAYS
TYPE	DOUBLE-DECKER
CAR NUMBER	399
DATE	1925
BUILDER	LEEDS CORPORATION TRAMWAYS
LENGTH	31½ FEET (9.6M)
WEIGHT	NOT KNOWN
SEATS	70
TRUCKS/WHEELS	ST

RIGHT

A towering car from this view, the warm light sets off original colors of chocolate, primrose, and white. Number 399 later served in dark blue and cream.

Representing a transitional type in British trolley evolution, number 399 sports a completely glassed-in upper deck. But examine the construction details, which would not seem out of place in cars dating from 25 years before, right down to the curved rocker panels. Apparently, this conservatism was the handiwork of the Leeds Tramways manager, who, ironically, had left his post before number 399 was complete.

Over the years, many later modifications transformed the car until its final use as a shunter and eventual decommission in 1957. At one point, wartime camouflage was even applied, but now the National Tramway Museum at Crich and the Leeds Tramway Historical Society have restored not only the classic bodywork, but also the original and attractive complex coach-and-four paint scheme.

BLACKPOOL, DOUBLE-DECKER NUMBER 40, 1926

SPECIFICATIONS

LIVERY
BLACKPOOL, ENGLAND

TYPE DOUBLE-DECKER

CAR NUMBER 40

DATE 1926

BUILDER BLACKPOOL
CORPORATION TRANSPORT

LENGTH
34 FEET (10.4M)

WEIGHT
NOT KNOWN

SEATS 78

TRUCKS/WHEELS DT

Open balconies on the upper decks of trolleys were popular in Britain, particularly in coastal towns like Blackpool. Although some of the trolleys of this generation were fitted with fully enclosed upper decks, Blackpool's number 40, built in 1926, never had this extra refinement. It was the last open-balconied car in regular service in Britain, operating until 1962 when it went to the National Tramway Museum, where it runs through the hills and fields around Matlock. As the 1930s began, newer types of cars started to replace those that seemed out of date, including number 40.

In Blackpool, 100 new streamliners were bought over the course of the decade. Other cities, though hampered by Depression budgets and, later, by preparations for the war, also struggled to modernize.

RIGHT

The bright red and cream livery contrasts with the green countryside near the National Tramway Museum. Most British trams had only a single trolley on the roof.

LONDON, DOUBLE-DECKER NUMBER 355, 1930

SPECIFICATIONS

LIVERY
LONDON TRANSPORT

TYPE DOUBLE-DECKER

CAR NUMBER 355

DATE 1930

BUILDER UNION CONSTRUCTION & FINANCE CO. LTD.

LENGTH
40½ FEET (12.3M)

WEIGHT
40,320LB. (18,327KG)

SEATS 64

TRUCKS/WHEELS DT

The perky, peaked cap over the motorman's platform made the Feltham-type trolley instantly recognizable. The Felthams, named after the London suburb in which they were built, also deserve recognition for their innovative design, which ushered in the streamline era that culminated with the American PCC design five years later. London Underground Group, which was responsible for the underground railroad as well as trolley transportation, broke new ground in the late 1920s and 1930s with a series of prototypes that eventually resulted in a production car possessing several advanced features. Among them were lightweight metal construction, which used the stair as part of the framework, magnetic braking, plush upholstered seating, and air-operated doors.

The Felthams, or UCC class cars as they were formally

ABOVE AND RIGHT

The upper deck seating was amazingly plush for its time. Compare it with the Irish Hill of Howth tram dating from 1900 (page 43).

known, served both London's MET (Metropolitan Electric Tramways) and LUT (London United Tramways) lines, as 100 machines were produced. Later, English Electric produced similar cars for Sunderland, Aberdeen, and Blackpool, where amazingly, they still run. They are large cars by British standards, with double trolleys and bogie trucks, and they can carry 84 people.

OPPOSITE

Shown in the sheds of the London Transport Museum with some of its fellow London trams in their traditional red, the double truck Feltham's large size is evident.

LIVERPOOL, DOUBLE-DECKER   NUMBER 869, 1936

SPECIFICATIONS

LIVERY
LIVERPOOL, ENGLAND

TYPE DOUBLE-DECKER

CAR NUMBER 869

DATE 1936

BUILDER
LIVERPOOL CORPORATION
PASSENGER TRANSPORT

LENGTH
37 FEET (11.3M)

WEIGHT
37,500LB. (17,045KG)

SEATS 78

TRUCKS/WHEELS DT

The fancifully, but aptly, named Green Goddess streamliners of Liverpool might have represented an appeal for divine intervention by desperate trolley operators. In small cities throughout Britain, trolley lines were giving up the ghost. In 1930 14,000 cars had been in operation, but by 1939 only 1,000 had been replaced by modern designs. The government actually opposed trolley operations, and only the major cities could afford to inaugurate programs to upgrade their systems.

Liverpool's streamliners, which were built in 1936 and 1937, stand up very well in comparison to their U.S. contemporary, the PCC car, except in terms of the number built. Large areas of curved glass gave the Liverpool "liner" even better aerodynamics than its U.S. counterpart. Heavyweight radial arm bogies, folding doors, and electro-pneumatic remote control were some of the mechanical innovations introduced by the Green Goddesses. A smaller two-axle version was given the catchy name "Baby Grand." Striking and stylish cars like these, and others such as the Glasgow "Coronation" cars and the Sheffield streamliners, were too few to help the beleaguered trolley systems which died out.

RIGHT

As it whispers through the snowy night, the Green Goddess definitely looks like an emissary from on high.

CHAPTER THREE

ALONG A PERFECT TRACK

THE TROLLEY CAR DOMINANT

Immediately before World War I, many types of large and efficient trolleys were developed, including the Peter Witt, the pay-as-you-enter car, and the center-entry car, all of which tried to control passenger entry and fare paying. Also discussed in this chapter are the ill-fated interurban trains, which were a peculiarly North American idea.

ALONG A PERFECT TRACK

Just as the last section of the previous chapter dealt exclusively with trolleys from Britain and Ireland, so the first part of this chapter looks at trolleys, from the rest of Europe. As we have noted, electric streetcars on the continent adhered to a consistent pattern and became standardized after the first decade of the century. The great majority underwent several modifications over a long life, and it is hard to find running examples without at least a windshield for the driver, even though most European trolleys made in 1905–15 had open platforms. Totally enclosed trolleys were introduced in more northerly countries for obvious reasons, and that is the way we find them today. Trolleys hitched to three or more trailers were also common, and this practice continues today. Because of the limitation on car length imposed by street layouts, four-wheelers were never really superseded by bogies, unlike in the U.S., where trolleys grew to huge lengths and weights, requiring the new patterns of entry and exit seen in the pay-as-you-enter cars and Peter Witts. A few cities, such as Paris and Lyon, had large center-entrance bogie cars, and Peter Witts ran in Venice. Compromise wheel layouts that used maximum traction trucks and odd six-wheel layouts were developed.

The distinction made in North America between city and interurban systems was blurred in Europe, and many streetcars ran between towns as country trolleys or suburban railroads. There the "interurban" trolleys were small, usually narrow gauge, meandering routes between small towns. Not much differentiated them from standard streetcars. They were often steam routes in the early days, and some still exist today. Only in eastern Europe have these lines survived, and it seems unlikely, given the apparently universal desire for road transportation, that these systems will survive.

Pacific Electric number 418.

Throughout the 1930s, most European tram systems were modernized incrementally, but municipal support remained strong, except in France, where the last Parisian trolley ran in 1938. Britain and the U.S. also began to lose interest in the trolley, only regaining some degree of enthusiasm as the new streamliners emerged. Most later European trolleys paid little heed to aerodynamics, although there were a few exceptions. Italy, always a leader in style, introduced modern cars in Turin and Milan, and even Germany, which was devoting its resources to military preparations, produced a few, such as the Essen streamliners of 1933 and the U.S. Bullet car-inspired Dresden "Grosshechtswagen," named because of its resemblance to a pike. But with a slow post-Depression recovery, followed by wartime privations, it was not until after 1945 that European trolleys flourished anew, unlike in Britain and the U.S., where the end of the war sounded the end of the trolley.

G RAZ, AUSTRIA, SINGLE TRUCK TRAM

SPECIFICATIONS

LIVERY
GRAZ, AUSTRIA

TYPE CLOSED

CAR NUMBER 120

DATE 1909

BUILDER GRAZER
WAGGON FABRIK

LENGTH
33½ FEET (10.2M)

WEIGHT
28,000LB. (12,727KG)

SEATS 18

TRUCKS/WHEELS ST

Little actually remains of the original car that was built for the city of Graz in 1909 by Grazer Waggon Fabrik. Its first incarnation had open platforms for the driver, but with glass windshields above the dashboard. At this time the nine cars in the batch were numbered from 80 to 88, with this car being the last. After nine years, number 88 received a new chassis and returned to service for a further 30 years. In 1918, after five years of disuse, new enclosed bodies were constructed for the six cars that remained of the original nine. The number 120 was assigned to it at this time.

RIGHT

The green valleys and vineyards of the Austrian state of Styria, of which Graz is capital, are echoed in the green livery of car number 120, which is pictured here at the National Capital Trolley Museum.

BELOW

The fanciful Styrian lion graces the sides of car number 120.

Although couplers were installed, number 120 always operated singly between 1955 and 1963. The National Capital Trolley Museum operates it in the livery of this period, and a fellow trolley, number 121, with a pantograph instead of a trolley pole, operates out of the Graz Tramway Museum. The Graz system, called the GVB, had a cream and green livery, and the trolleys sported the fanciful Styrian panther of the city coat of arms, which dates from the 13th century.

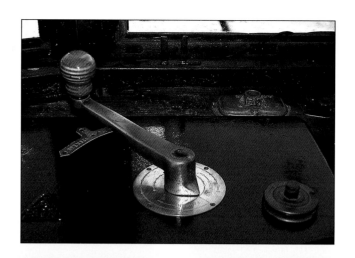

LEFT AND ABOVE *Inside the closed car (left), alternating dark and light banded wood sets a lighter tone. The top picture is the meticulously maintained Elin controller. The lengthwise seating is typical of these narrow trolleys.*

SPECIFICATIONS

LIVERY
VIENNA, AUSTRIA

TYPE CLOSED

CAR NUMBER 6062

DATE 1910

BUILDER GRAZ WORKS

LENGTH
34FT. 7IN. (10.6M)

WEIGHT
29,000LB. (13,182KG)

SEATS 22

TRUCKS/WHEELS ST

When they were built in 1910, these cars were the first in Vienna to have closed platforms. Car number 2249, as it was then, underwent a complete rebuilding in 1935, but retains most of the features of the original, except for a small speed increase. The distinguishing features include two axles with a 11 feet 8 inches (3.6m) wheelbase, eight windows on each side, and double doors, and these remained remarkably constant among all the trolleys produced for Vienna. By 1962 car number 6062 had become a snowplow and worked as such for another seven years until it was sent to the National Capital Trolley Museum in Washington, D.C. The red and white colors of the Austrian flag are echoed in the livery, and the white cross on a red field echoes the shield of Vienna, which is also the emblem of the city's transportation system.

RIGHT

Red Viennese paintwork glows in the dark sheds of the National Capital Trolley Museum. Number 6062 has been restored to its appearance in around 1935.

RIGHT AND BELOW

Polished brass handles helped boarders through the double doors (right). The headlight detail and electrical take-off, which was used when running in trains are shown below.

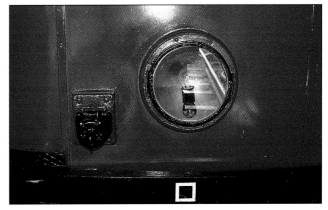

GOTHENBURG, SINGLE TRUCK NUMBER 71, 1912

SPECIFICATIONS

LIVERY
GOTHENBURG, SWEDEN

TYPE CLOSED STEEL

CAR NUMBER 71

DATE 1912

BUILDER ASEA

LENGTH
33¾ FEET (10.3M)

WEIGHT
27,500LB. (12,500KG)

SEATS 20

TRUCKS/WHEELS ST

Still in need of much restoration work, this Swedish trolley reveals quite a sleek interior as it is nosed part way out of the shed for the photo session. When it was completed in 1912, it must have seemed to the citizens of Gothenburg to be the last word in swift transportation. Differing only in detail from most single-truck European trolleys of the period, number 71 is heavily built for use in pulling trains of cars, and it is totally enclosed, as a U.S. car of that time would not have been. Notice how narrow this standard gauge car appears because of the minimal overhang of the sides of the body, and the visual effect caused by the three high, narrow panes of glass of the windshield. The expansive panes of plate glass for the passengers' windows were very modern, as was the use of regenerative braking through the motors. But the hand brake is a huge railroad style vertical wheel, unlike the gooseneck style preferred in the U.S.

The typical Swedish concern for clear markings, including the color-coded side panels, back-lit nose display, and unusual rotating four-sided destination board above the platform roof, is evident. The livery is blue and cream, with the coat of arms of the city of Gothenburg, which portrays the Lion of Folkungar holding the three crowns of Sweden.

LEFT

Barely able to move under its own power, number 71 sidled between the sheds of the Connecticut Museum, giving only a glimpse of the exterior details.

ABOVE

Number 71 has an extremely simple and direct single truck chassis.

*Stark simplicity is the hallmark of
the narrow-nosed Gothenburg
trolley.*

*The original, unrestored AEG
controller and mechanical
braking hand wheel. The interior
finish is in need of much work.*

DÜSSELDORF, SINGLE-TRUCK TRAM NUMBER 955, 1928

SPECIFICATIONS	
LIVERY	DÜSSELDORF, GERMANY
TYPE	CLOSED WOOD
CAR NUMBER	955
DATE	1928
BUILDER	SCHONDORFF
LENGTH	34FT. 9IN. (10.6M)
WEIGHT	30,000LB. (13,636KG)
SEATS	26
TRUCKS/WHEELS	ST

OPPOSITE

Off on an early spring jaunt through the woods around the National Capital Trolley Museum, number 955 demonstrates the pantograph that was standard on many later European trams.

LEFT

Pristine paintwork and running gear mark this as a first-class restoration.

In the stark, creamy white of the Rheinbahn, as Dusseldorf's transportation company is known to the locals, number 955 looks surprisingly modern for a car built in 1928. This is even more remarkable considering that the Bauhaus-type styling of the metal-clad body conceals one of the last wooden-bodied cars to be built in Germany. The wide doors made loading passengers easy, and the tram was prized for its riding comfort. The 52 cars in this series remained in service until the late 1960s, when they were replaced by articulated cars built by the same parent company, Duewag, that had built number 955.

The discreetly marked number 955 seems almost petite, but it is in fact 7½ feet (2.3m) wide and nearly 35 feet (10.6m) long with a weight of 15 tons. There are 26 seats in the darkly varnished wood interior, and visibility is superb through the huge plate glass windows.

RIGHT AND FAR RIGHT

The original Siemens controller and the hand-operated bell on the platform roof.

LEFT

The position of the Rheinbahn logo and markings are typically discreet.

RHEINISCHE BAHNGESELLSCHAFT A.G.

GHENT, SIX-WHEEL TRAM NUMBER 324

RIGHT

Number 324 from Ghent shows off its six-wheel turning abilities in this 1972 photograph. Note also the use of a bow collector instead of trolley pole.

If two axles are too small and four axles are too bulky and expensive, maybe three axles are the answer. Through the use of sleight of hand involving a central "link axle," a car using six wheels could be made to go around curves and return all axles to a parallel position, as long as the central axle stayed fixed. With unsuccessful experiments in Plauen, Germany, and Leeds, England, at the turn of the century, both the U.S. and Britain disdained the six-wheeler, but European cities such as Ghent, Belgium; Basel, Switzerland; and Lille, France; found the combination of size, smooth ride and economy unbeatable.

The six-wheelers of Ghent, which were still running in the city center when this photograph was taken in 1972, were smaller than the cars used in Basel, and, apart from the six wheels, were indistinguishable from most European trams. Maintenance problems kept other cities from adopting them, and most have long since disappeared.

HANOVER, RURAL TRAM

SPECIFICATIONS

LIVERY
HANOVER, GERMANY

TYPE CLOSED

CAR NUMBER 219

DATE 1930

BUILDER HANOVERSCHE
WAGGONFABRIK "HANA"

LENGTH
34½ FEET (10.5M)

WEIGHT
27,720LB. (12,600KG)

SEATS 26

TRUCKS/WHEELS DT

Midway between US interurbans, and typical city trams, this rural tram from Hanover, Germany, operated over routes that were quite long in European terms. The route shown on the oversized destination box – Barsinghausen – was 17 miles (28km). Although it is still a two-axle car, shown here with two trailers as it is preserved at Wehmingen, these metal-bodied, standard gauge urban trams date from 1928. An underfloor controller and electric rail brakes are modern touches. One route ran larger bogie cars. All these routes were gradually phased out in the 1950s, with the last running in 1961. Freight services on these lines, which once carried some of the heaviest traffic in Europe, were stopped in 1953.

RIGHT

Hanover train number 219 and two trailers, now in limbo at Wehmingen. Notice the original large sun visor over the windshield, and the pantograph collector.

GIJÓN, RURAL TRAM NUMBER 15–22, 1940S

RIGHT

Hundreds of miles from Belgium, this Vicinal (or SNCV) type N pulls a short train through the rainy countryside of northern Spain.

Shown emerging from a tunnel on its run from Gijon to Avilés across the Cabo de Penas in Spain, the ex-SNCV class N was about the ultimate in the standard European tram that was used for long-distance service. The Belgian SNCV, or Vicinal, was a state-sponsored monopoly that eventually controlled the largest single tram system in the world, with almost 3,000 miles (4,800km) of track at its peak in 1940. In the 1930s, Belgium adopted larger bogie cars as standard, culminating in the type N of the early 1940s. Pleasantly rounded and streamlined in shape, they could achieve 45mph (72kph). Each car could carry 100 people under the power of two 85 horsepower motors. As Belgium scaled back its rural tram system in the late 1960s, some of these cars went to northern Spain and did a stint with the Carreno Railway in Gijón.

Today, it is hard to imagine any other fare-paying method than giving the money for the fare to the driver. Almost all local buses are one-man operated, and it is almost as if there was never any other way. Who needs a conductor?

In Montreal in 1904, the idea that a passenger should pay when getting onto a trolley or tram was revolutionary, but by 1915 the idea had spread to Toronto and then to most parts of North America. Although TCR number 55 still used a conductor, the stage was set in later cars for front entry and one-man operation. Open cars, of course, did not lend themselves to the new pay-as-you-enter (PAYE) method, which was another factor leading to their phase-out.

TORONTO PAYE NUMBER 55, 1915

SPECIFICATIONS

LIVERY
TORONTO TRANSPORTATION COMMISSION

TYPE WOOD PAYE

CAR NUMBER 55

DATE 1915

BUILDER PRESTON

LENGTH
34FT. 8IN. (10.6M)

WEIGHT
29,400LB. (13,364KG)

SEATS 32

TRUCKS/WHEELS ST

On double-ended cars, such as number 55, the large platforms and double doors allowed passengers to board quickly at either end. Although car number 55 had a smooth arch roof and the modern pay-as-you-enter layout, its wooden matchboard construction, single truck, two-motor chassis and, especially, lack of air brakes, branded it as hopelessly obsolete by 1926. Removed from revenue operations, but saved from the scrapyard, it served 30 more years as a snow scraper.

RIGHT

The front view of number 55 reveals the mixture of new arch roof and old wood matchboard construction that cut short its career.

ALONG A PERFECT TRACK

Peter Witt has earned a minor sort of fame. The commissioner of street railways in Cleveland, Ohio, immediately after World War I, Witt designed a fare-paying scheme and car layout that became standard among many companies as they sought the most efficient ways of getting passsengers on and off the cars. This type of car and its cousin, the nearside car, brought people into a large holding area in the front of the car and let them leave in the center where the conductor stood. The best seats were in the rear, and to get to them you had to pass the conductor and pay your fare. This logical pattern reduced boarding delays greatly, and so Peter Witt-type cars spread throughout the world. Toronto, Buffalo, Baltimore, and Philadelphia in North America had them, but Milan was probably the last city to use them in large numbers, which it still does.

Apart from their loading patterns, the Peter Witt cars, particularly the smaller, later versions, used the most modern techniques to reduce weight and to increase comfort and safety. The cars had such features as steel arch roof bodies with improved ventilation, air-operated doors, and improved motors and performance.

TORONTO, PETER WITT NUMBER 2894, 1923

SPECIFICATIONS

LIVERY	TORONTO TRANSPORTATION COMMISSION
TYPE	P. WITT
CAR NUMBER	2894
DATE	1923
BUILDER	OTTAWA CAR MANUFACTURING CO.
LENGTH	47 FEET (14.3M)
WEIGHT	39,700LB. (18,045KG)
SEATS	51
TRUCKS/WHEELS	DT

LEFT

This view of the rear of the single-ended car shows the better seats that were available there. Bench seats at the front encouraged people to move to the center and pay their fares.

This streetside view of a Peter Witt hides the center doors that were a trademark of the design, but shows the clean lines that were the last word in 1923.

The driver's station in number 2894. Glowing coils on the left show that the power is on.

The very latest in the art of trolley design, c.1923, number 2894 was built by Ottawa Car Manufacturing Co. to Canadian Car & Foundry specifications for use by the Toronto Transportation Commission. Gone was the clerestory roof; in its place was smooth decking and ocean liner-type ventilators. The ribbed bumper, whose horizontal strips look very Art Deco, was actually the "anti-climber." In a collision, the grooves were to prevent one trolley from riding up on another and "telescoping" into the passenger area, the most horrendous kind of accident a streetcar could have.

Although it was known as a "small Witt," because it was 5 feet (1.5m) shorter and more lightly built than the "large Witt" equivalents, thus shaving nearly 10,000 pounds (4,500kg) off gross weight, it was every bit as wide in the beam. So wide in fact, that all Toronto's trolley tracks had to be ripped up and respaced to allow these behemoths to pass each other.

The car shown in these photographs was used in Toronto for trolley tours and charter work until 1986, when the Halton County Radial Railway Museum acquired the last of the "small Witts."

BALTIMORE, PETER WITT

SPECIFICATIONS

LIVERY	BALTIMORE UNITED RAILWAYS CO.
TYPE	P. WITT
CAR NUMBER	6119
DATE	1930
BUILDER	J.G. BRILL
LENGTH	46 FEET (14M)
WEIGHT	38,500LB. (17,500KG)
SEATS	52
TRUCKS/WHEELS	DT

The Peter Witt system of fare collection was patented, and the Baltimore United Railways Co. duly paid the royalties, but cars like number 6119 ran almost from the beginning as one-man, front-entry vehicles. The economic conditions of the Depression finally forced the conductor from the scene. The 150 cars themselves, the largest purchase by Baltimore since 1919, came from the J. G. Brill & Cincinnati Car Co. These last were the final cars ever to be produced by the old Cincinnati firm, another casualty of the Depression.

Running from 1930 until 1954, these Peter Witts represented the pinnacle of streetcar design, until they were supplanted by the world-beating PCC. The interiors were comfortable, if institutional, and in a jack-rabbit start, trolleys like number 6119 could out-accelerate most automobiles of the time. The wide gauge, 5 feet 4½ inches (1.64m) which was shared by all Baltimore streetcars, was a vestige of an old 1859 ordinance requiring tracks to allow use by horse-drawn wagons, and it was wider than any other American tram system. This, combined with a length of 46 feet (14m), made number 6119 capable of moving a large number of people.

Here is a car for the big city. The typical center doors were used as exits, although never as Peter Witt intended. One-man operation was the rule.

LEFT AND ABOVE

The driver now has a seat (left)! The fare collection box, which was used until the 1950s all over North America, had a hypnotic, magical effect as it clicked and swallowed the coins. The rear seat (above) folds down to reveal emergency controls for reverse operation.

The interurban trolley seemed such a powerful idea, particularly in the American Midwest. The steam railroads had no interest in connecting small towns with any kind of frequent service, for the large locomotives took forever to stop and get up to speed again. Self-powered trolleys, on the other hand, were perfectly suited to quick stops and starts, smooth acceleration, and long runs at high speed. Indeed, the later American interurban cars appeared unstoppable – majestic machines that could out-accelerate a steam locomotive and, given a favorable headwind, out-race an airplane. They were an intimidating 3 feet (91cm) higher than a streetcar and twice as heavy.

The technology was easily adaptable to long distances. Using low-loss, high-voltage lines to transmit the power and step-down transformers spaced along the track to feed the accustomed 600 volts to the car, power losses were kept to the minimum. It is true, however, that the first of the interurbans, in Sandusky, Ohio, and Portland, Oregon, in 1893, folded quickly, largely because hardware and reliability still presented problems. Nevertheless, pressure mounted for the construction of new lines.

Not only did large stretches of the country need tying together, but people were convinced that their town was "nowhere," a backwater, unless it had an interurban connection. So, the networks grew and grew from the Midwest, where Ohio alone had nearly 3,000 miles (4,800km) of track and it was possible to take a 349km (217 mile) trip between Cincinnati and Toledo. The northeast and south also fell under their spell, with property values up everywhere, and the giant railroad companies started to acquire control of the upstart interurbans. In the west, where such men as H. E. Huntington and his Pacific Electric cars were building furiously, it was possible in Los

Angeles in 1905 to make a profit of 60 percent on property held for just a month. By 1913 plans were complete to construct a grand interurban connection 750 miles (1,200km) long from New York to Chicago, which would be called the "Air Line."

Two beautifully appointed cars were built and stock was sold, but the bubble was ready to burst. It cost more and more to bring each new passenger into the system, and as city centers grew more congested, the 60–70mph (95–110kph) speedsters had to crawl through town. Most ominous of all, roads were improving, and interurban passengers grew ever more vulnerable to the siren call of the automobile. Even buses made more sense economically. The interurbans had been magnificent machines though, in their short golden age, with names like the "Orange Limited," the "Muncie Meteor," and the "Red Devil." They are all gone now. The only remaining interurban run in the U.S. is the South Shore, Indiana, line, which uses modern equipment. As we discovered in our search for preserved cars, few even went to museums. The heavy steel bodies were worth too much as scrap!

The electric interurban was a rarity in Britain. Those that were built seemed to exist to take tourists to country destinations; one such was the Manx Electric tramway on the Isle of Man. The rest of Europe, as we have seen, took a totally different route. One exception, not dissimilar to the U.S. concept, was in Germany, where the Hanover "Hildesheimer Flyer" ran; this had the large, double-truck wheels, luxurious fittings, and heavy, ironclad construction of its American cousins.

CHICAGO, INTERURBAN NUMBER 315, 1909

SPECIFICATIONS

LIVERY
CHICAGO, AURORA
& ELGIN

TYPE INTERURBAN WOOD

CAR NUMBER 315

DATE 1909

BUILDER KUHLMAN

LENGTH
54 FEET (16.5M)

WEIGHT
100,000LB. (45,454KG)

SEATS 52

TRUCKS/WHEELS DT

RIGHT

It is hard to grasp today how awesome these cars once seemed. As number 315 inches out of its barn, it resembles an aging caged panther.

RIGHT

Just give number 315, even now,
a few miles of straight track, and
the power would return: 35 tons
hurtling along at 80mph
(128kph).

LEFT AND
ABOVE

An archeological dig is underway,
as paint is peeled away and old
wood and brass fixtures are
restored to their former
splendor.

The Chicago, Aurora & Elgin took delivery of this, one of the last wood-bodied interurbans, in 1909. Built by Kuhlman, a less well-known Cleveland firm, it was the last word in speed and power, and could cruise at 80mph (128kph), a speed not reached by the fastest airplanes until 1911. In 1940, in the spirit of the times, C, A & E decided to do some modernization, although today we would call what they did desecration. Arched, stained glass transom windows were covered over outside; inside, they received a coat of bright blue paint, as did all the wood paneling, carvings, and brasswork. Recognizing comfort when they saw it, however, the leather seats and rest room, with its oval window, remained. Outside, the match-boarded bodywork, huge headlight, and upright brass air whistle give clues to her vintage. In this condition, number 315 soldiered on until 1959, leading the last run of the Chicago, Aurora & Elgin on July 3 of that year.

SPECIFICATIONS	
LIVERY	MONTREAL & SOUTHERN COUNTIES RAILROAD
TYPE	INTERURBAN
CAR NUMBER	107
DATE	1912
BUILDER	OTTAWA CAR CO.
LENGTH	49FT. 4IN. (15M)
WEIGHT	57,000LB. (25,909KG)
SEATS	32
TRUCKS/WHEELS	DT

Interurbans were called "radials" in Canada because they spread out from city hubs in a web-like radial pattern. Montreal and Southern Counties Railroad number 107 is a classic wooden-bodied interurban car, which ran a suburban service between Montreal and towns on the Saint Lawrence River. These routes were somewhat shorter than it was designed for, and for this reason the baggage compartment became a smoking area. By 1912, when number 107 emerged from the Ottawa Car Co.'s factory, all the features of the North American interurban were in place, the most prominent of these being the Pullman-style, or railroad roof, which blended into the rounded nose where a huge, searchlight-like headlamp perched. If the rail lines ran parallel to a main road, the lamp would usually be roof-mounted so that it would not blind oncoming motorists. An unusual feature is the truck-mounted pilot or cow catcher. Unlike number 107, most later interurbans had a ribbed bumper or anti-climber, as mentioned before. The fast interurbans were particularly susceptible to collisions, and passenger fatalities resulting from the "telescoping" of cars in a pile-up were not uncommon. Also lacking are the wooden strips across the roof ends, and the "roof mat," which could protect against the trolley pole crashing through the roof if the spring failed; a common occurrence. Inside, passenger comforts were catered for – only 32 widely spaced seats are provided in a car almost 50 feet (15m) long. The clerestory and upper sash windows are stained glass. A single driver could operate trains of this type of car, an important feature on many high-traffic interurban routes.

RIGHT

This end of number 107 is windowless because it was meant to be a baggage area on long routes.

BELOW

The huge, yellow-tinged headlight, used as a fog light, dominates the front end.

PACIFIC ELECTRIC, INTERURBAN Number 418, 1913

SPECIFICATIONS	
LIVERY PACIFIC ELECTRIC	
TYPE INTERURBAN	
CAR NUMBER 418	
DATE 1913	
BUILDER PULLMAN	
LENGTH 72FT. 4IN. (22.1M)	
WEIGHT 125,660LB. (57,118KG)	
SEATS 80	
TRUCKS/WHEELS DT	

The baleful stare of the two huge porthole windows could lead one to mistake this car for a railroad passenger coach, but this is definitely a trolley – part of the "World's Biggest Interurban" line, the Pacific Electric. Almost 1,000 miles (1,600km) of track formed the backbone of the city sprawl that is Los Angeles and its suburbs. Almost all of it was put there through the determination and deal-making abilities of Henry E. Huntington, president of Pacific Electric in the 1900s. The "Big Red" cars of Pacific Electric went where he decreed the track should run, and to a great extent, Los Angeles has the size and shape it does because of him.

Number 418 started its life with Southern Pacific in the San Francisco Bay area, where it met the Oakland Ferry, among other duties. The rail-style couplers at front and rear and the pass-through doors on the platform ends allowed it to be used in trains up to 10 cars long. Pullman and the St. Louis Car Co. built many cars similar to it until the 1930s, and in World War II, they were pressed into service to transport Los Angeles shipyard and aircraft workers. No real "Big Red" cars survive, so number 418 has been painted to represent one of the vanished hundreds. Inside the car, wooden paneling and chandeliers have vanished, to be replaced by the sanitized, enameled look of modern institutional decor that became common in the 1920s, although the seats are more comfortable than they look. The driver's platform, in contrast, is as starkly functional as a World War I U-boat.

ABOVE

A "Big Red" car – Pacific Electric number 418 in its element, poised to streak across the California scrub lands.

LEFT

The unusual fare register is clock-like object on bulkhead.

ABOVE, LEFT AND FAR LEFT

The driver's cabin with a front "porthole" (left). The primitive switches (above) have served for 80 years. Note the controller key. Exterior detailing (far left) of the driver's cabin.

BRITISH COLUMBIA, INTERURBAN NUMBER 1225, 1913

SPECIFICATIONS

LIVERY
BRITISH COLUMBIA
ELECTRIC RAILWAY

TYPE INTERURBAN STEEL

CAR NUMBER 1225

DATE 1913

BUILDER
ST. LOUIS CAR CO.

LENGTH
51 FT. 4 IN. (15.7 M)

WEIGHT
70,800 LB. (32,181 KG)

SEATS 48

TRUCKS/WHEELS DT

Canada's west coast is vast, seemingly perfect for development of interurban or "radial" railroads, and there were eventually hundreds of cars on its routes. Nevertheless, in all of Canada, there were never more than 850 miles (1,370km) of interurban track. Ordered from the St. Louis Car Co. in 1913, car number 1225 ran in and around Vancouver. Because it used a mix of wood and steel construction, it was known as a composite car. New features, such as simplified, large windows and an uncluttered, arch roof, are mixed with old-style narrow doors and matchboard wood sides. As these photographs show, the wooden bodywork of the car is desperately in need of restoration, although the mechanical gear is in good shape.

ABOVE

The focused heat from the powerful headlamp can be felt from 6 feet (2m) away.

RIGHT

Although it may be mechanically perfect underneath, number 1225's bodywork needs much careful restoration.

LEFT AND BELOW

The paintwork (bottom) shows the ravages of the strong desert sun. Reconstruction work on the interior is just beginning (below), and the smoking section seats (left) would encourage you to give up the weed forever!

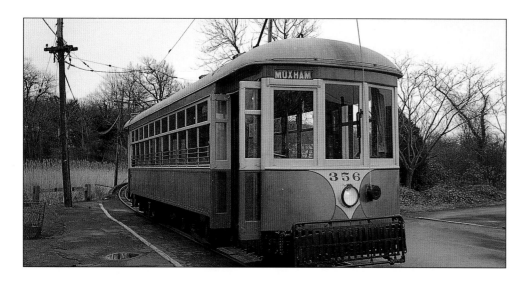

Lightweight car number 356
from the Johnstown Traction Co.

Despite the huge growth in the American trolley industry in the 1900s, by the early years of World War I some route systems were struggling. Not only had Henry Ford's Model-T and its ilk put millions of ordinary people on the road, but costs and wages were rising as passenger numbers levelled off. The industry, with some equipment now 15 or 20 years old, was also suffering from what would today be called an infrastructure problem. Therefore, when Charles Birney designed a new type of car for Stone & Webster, a large traction company combine that promised to solve these problems, manufacturers and transit companies alike rushed to place orders.

The new Birney Safety Car was a clever mixture of modern and antique. Reaching back to the days of the horse-drawn car, when some companies introduced small one-horse cars called "bobtails" as an economy move, the Birney reverted to a short wheelbase, single-truck layout for minimum weight and low unit cost. New technology included the smooth arch roof and a stressed skin construction that routed structural loads through external body panels, thereby reducing the weight and bulk of the frame. A key strategy was one-man operation, which was achieved by the use of the new deadman switch on the controller and by an interlock on the doors so that the car could not move if they were open. The smaller wheels and high-efficiency compact motors allowed for a lower overall height. On paper, at least, it seemed a sure winner, and thousands of Birney Safety Cars were made between 1916 and 1921.

Although the wide, low, well-rounded design gave the appearance of competence, in practice they fell short. The passengers were the first to notice: a rocking, porpoising ride because of the short wheelbase and light weight led the public to christen the cars "Galloping Gerties" and "Rocking Horses." Because only one of the two doors would usually be in use at a time, boarding congestion was unceasing. The companies found that their problems had been only temporarily staved off by the new cars. Although possibly understandable, it was both shortsighted and naive to believe that a transformation in public attitudes as fundamental as that brought by the automobile could be countered by some tinkering with the hardware. After all, in Europe the standard tram was basically similar in concept to the Birney and has met the needs of city dwellers there for a century because the car posed little threat to the established tram lines until well after World War II. In Britain, however, something similar to the Safety Car appeared. This was the Raworth Regenerative Demi-car, which even with some advanced features and a memorable name, was less successful than the Birney. Transportation companies in Britain clung to the big double-decker formula – even the buses that supplanted trams were double-deckers.

PACIFIC ELECTRIC, BIRNEY NUMBER 331, 1918

SPECIFICATIONS

LIVERY	PACIFIC ELECTRIC
TYPE	BIRNEY SAFETY
CAR NUMBER	331
DATE	1918
BUILDER	J. G. BRILL
LENGTH	27¾ FEET (8.5M)
WEIGHT	14,700LB. (6,681KG)
SEATS	32
TRUCKS/WHEELS	ST

LEFT

The wide, simple look of a shoe box on wheels characterizes the typical Birney Safety Car.

BELOW

Concern for minimum weight continues inside, leading to the rather spare "little red schoolhouse" look.

ABOVE

A metal skin with prominent rivets was an important structural load-bearing element, which helped to reduce the weight of frame members.

After many years toiling on the Inland Empire line, this little Birney Safety Car went on to a brief movie career, the high point of which was a cameo role in *Singing in the Rain*, when Gene Kelly got to dance on the roof. After that, the car lingered on the back lots of Warner Bros. until it was rescued by the Orange Empire Railway Museum in Perris, California.

Built in 1918 by J. G. Brill in the short heyday of the Birney Safety Car, number 331 at least had four doors to ease loading and exiting, but otherwise had the loping gait of all this breed. It saw service on local lines – Long Beach, Pasadena, and eastward on the Inland Empire line – wearing the now-restored spiffy red of Pacific Electric.

YORK RAILWAYS, CURVED-SIDE CAR NUMBER 163, 1924

SPECIFICATIONS	
LIVERY	YORK RAILWAYS, PENNSYLVANIA
TYPE	CITY CAR
CAR NUMBER	163
DATE	1924
BUILDER	J. G. BRILL
LENGTH	42¼ FEET (12.9M)
WEIGHT	36,000LB. (16,364KG)
SEATS	40
TRUCKS/WHEELS	DT

Looking in surprisingly good condition for a trolley that survived a flood while serving as a summer cottage, number 163 of York Railways has undergone a 17-year restoration at the Rockhill Trolley Museum. Before then, the car had been lived in for 33 years after York Railways changed its trolleys for buses in 1939. An unusual car in many ways, it is not a true Safety Car, being instead one of only five curved-side cars built by J. G. Brill before another firm, claiming ownership of the design, forced Brill to stop production. The odd arched windows conceal pockets for the unusual air-operated sliding doors. The remains of all five cars have been used in restoring the cherry wood interior and rattan seats. The livery of orange, cream, and maroon is that used in its last years.

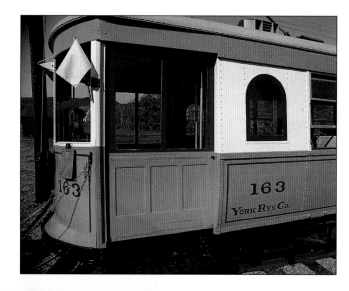

ABOVE

The archaic, curved side panels caused trouble for J. G. Brill, which was accused of plagiarizing the design.

BELOW AND RIGHT

The flip-over seats (right) and the cherry wood driver's cab (below).

OPPOSITE

Simple unique windows are highlighted by the paintwork.

JOHNSTOWN TRACTION CO., LIGHTWEIGHT

NUMBER 356, 1926

SPECIFICATIONS

LIVERY	JOHNSTOWN TRACTION COMPANY, PENNSYLVANIA
TYPE	LIGHTWEIGHT
CAR NUMBER	356
DATE	1926
BUILDER	ST. LOUIS CAR CO.
LENGTH	41 FEET (12.5M)
WEIGHT	38,000LB. (17,273KG)
SEATS	44
TRUCKS/WHEELS	DT

ABOVE AND RIGHT

A detail of the headlights (above) picks up the bird-like quality of Johnstown Traction Co.'s livery. The warm tones used in the interior (right) generate feelings of comfort and welcome.

In the bright orange-yellow and white "songbird" livery of the Johnstown Traction Co., Pennsylvania, is the lightweight Safety Car of 1926. Lightweight as used here is a relative term, because these cars weighed around 19 tons. Putting on a brave show in the face of spreading competition from buses, cars, and even "jitney buses," which were private cars used as pirate-style buses along trolley routes, these trolleys had a host of improvements under the skin. Although number 356 was built by the St. Louis Car Co. the design originated in the Birney Safety Car of Charles Birney, dating from 1915.

To eliminate the earlier four-wheelers' atrocious riding qualities, the Pennsylvania car is a larger, double-ended, double-truck layout, and it still retains the safety features that allowed one-man operation. The car could not be moved with the doors open, and a deadman switch stopped the car safely if the driver were incapacitated. Topping it all off with a smooth, silver, domed roof, Johnstown Traction's number 356 and its fellows brought a needed jolt of modernity to the struggling trolley business. Cars like these filled the gap until the middle of the "Streamlined Decade" and the advent of PCC car designs.

OPPOSITE

The livery of Johnstown Traction Co. brings a bit of color to the bleak, early spring Connecticut landscape near the aptly named Shore Line Trolley Museum.

MONTREAL TRAMWAYS, LIGHTWEIGHT
NUMBER 2001, 1929

SPECIFICATIONS	
LIVERY MONTREAL TRAMWAYS	
TYPE LIGHTWEIGHT STEEL	
CAR NUMBER 2001	
DATE 1929	
BUILDER CANADIAN CAR & FOUNDRY	
LENGTH 41FT. 2IN. (12.6M)	
WEIGHT 38,000LB. (17,273KG)	
SEATS 32	
TRUCKS/WHEELS DT	

This unremarkable looking lightweight car comes from Canada. When Canadian Car & Foundry built number 2001 in 1929, it was a single-ended car, but by 1933 it had been converted to a double-ended arrangement for use on suburban lines. Many of these lines typically did not have loops or Ys to allow turnaround, hence the need for driver's positions on both ends of the car. Number 2001 and a twin, number 1972, also to be found in the Branford Collection, worked all their lives for Montreal Tramways.

ABOVE

The ubiquitous rattan seats were used for a minimal, but comfortable interior. Are today's fiberglass shells any better?

RIGHT

The unrestored front end of car number 2001, which shows the battered metalwork of a hard-fought 60-year life on Montreal's streets.

LEFT AND BELOW

The wide windshield arc (left) is apparent, but the destination blinds seem a bit undersized. The seated driver commands a cluttered, but basically simple, set of controls (below) including hand brake wheel, controller, and air brake.

NEW YORK, LIGHTWEIGHT   NUMBER 629, 1939

Straightforward lettering and signs give travelers all the information they need. Compare this with same line's earlier car number 220 (see page 19).

Worlds away from New York's 3rd Avenue, car number 629 now runs along the East Haven River in Connecticut.

SPECIFICATIONS

LIVERY	3RD AVENUE RAILWAY CO.
TYPE	LIGHTWEIGHT
CAR NUMBER	629
DATE	1939
BUILDER	3RD AVENUE RAILWAY
LENGTH	46½ FEET (14.2M)
WEIGHT	37,590LB. (17,086KG)
SEATS	46
TRUCKS/WHEELS	DT

The Marshall Plan worked many miracles in a devastated postwar Europe, and one of the strangest must have been the shipment of 40 New York City streetcars to Vienna, Austria, where they served for 20 years. New York had recently made the transition to an all-bus surface transportation system and was only too glad to be rid of the cars.

The cars had been built less than 10 years before by the 3rd Avenue Railway Co. in its midtown Manhattan factory, to the lightweight safety car standard originated by Birney 20 years before, and this made them the last conventional – i.e., non-streamlined – trolleys ever built in the U.S. New York was one of the only big cities not to buy PCC cars for its fleet. Fiorello LaGuardia, mayor of New York at that time, wanted to abandon old-fashioned streetcars for the more appealing buses, but budget considerations meant that stop-gap new purchases had to be made until the proposed transition to buses was made in 1960. No money was available for PCCs, so the privately owned 3rd Avenue Railway Co. built its own, using re-manufactured trucks and frames combined with new bodies. The not unpleasant, boxy shape was similar to a series of aluminum-bodied cars that had been built a few years before. When they were running in the city, a conduit "plow" was used so that no trolley pole marred the smooth, arched roof. Vienna ran these cars with pantograph current collectors. Number 629 was, at that time, numbered 4329. Now the Branford Museum has restored it to the red and cream livery of the 3rd Avenue Railway Co., and the X-marked route placard stands for – what else? – Crosstown.

CHAPTER FOUR

DREAMLINERS

PCCs AND OTHER STREAMLINERS

To reverse the downturn in their fortunes caused by the automobile and bus traffic, the trolley companies introduced a new streamlined trolley, and it became the standard for the trolley car of the future. These PCC cars and others, such as the Brill-liner, were only partly successful, but many are in service even today.

RIGHT

*The front end of the Philadelphia
Bullet car compared with a later
PCC.*

For a trolley car designed by a committee, the PCC stream-liner was overwhelmingly successful. It was named after the Electric Railway Presidents' Conference Committee. Production totaled 5,000 in the Americas, with 15,000 to 20,000 more coming from factories in eastern Europe. Hundreds still run on routes throughout the world 60 years after their debut in 1934 – Newark, New Jersey, runs them, as do Philadelphia and San Francisco; The Hague has just retired them, but many still pull their weight elsewhere in Europe and in Latin America.

The committee began work in 1929, and after five years' effort, there was a ground-up redesign of every component of the streetcar. Mechanical improvements concentrated on smooth, rapid acceleration and a whisper-quiet ride. As for the exterior skin, it was to be expected that the "dream streetcar" would take the aerodynamically inspired streamliner shape. Steam locomotives of the day received the same treatment by industrial designers such as Bel Geddes and Loewy, as did many other vehicles and appliances. Experimental railroad locomotives in Italy and Britain, moreover, had predated the PCC liners by a few years, and in 1931 J. G. Brill had produced a series of 10 high-speed rail cars known as the Bullet cars, with radically streamlined noses. Although they were far from the perfect teardrop shape, the PCC prototypes resembled nothing else then running on U.S. trolley tracks. The St. Louis Car Co. and Pullman-Standard rushed them into production. As a fitting inaugural gesture for this new breed of trolley, Frank Sprague, the man who had started the whole business in 1877, rode in a prototype PCC car shortly before his death.

PHILADELPHIA, BULLET CAR Number 205, 1931

LIVERY	PHILADELPHIA & WESTERN
TYPE	BULLET CAR
CAR NUMBER	205
DATE	1931
BUILDER	J. G. BRILL
LENGTH	55FT. 2IN. (16.8M)
WEIGHT	52,000LB. (23,636KG)
SEATS	52
TRUCKS/WHEELS	DT

RIGHT

Showing its wind-tunnel styling mainly around the nose, the Bullet car cleaves the air with its prow.

Probably the first trolley ever to be tested in a wind tunnel, the Bullet car was J. G. Brill's bid to revolutionize the high-speed interurban market. The car was the first American trolley to sell streamlining to the traveling public, and as such, the Bullet car was definitely a precursor of the PCC. In 1931 this striking car was introduced after tests by the University of Michigan's aerodynamicist, Professor Felix Pawlowski, showed a 42 percent increase in efficiency resulting from its streamlined shape and aluminum body. One of the largest customers was the Philadelphia & Western, which placed them in service at the end of 1931. Even as the Depression decimated the inter-urban lines, P&W traffic increased, for the public loved the new cars and their speeds of 85mph (137kph). P&W's successor, SEPTA, continued to run them as part of its Red Arrow lines, where they spent a phenomenal 60 years on the main line. These particular Bullet cars never ran as trolleys, using a third rail exclusively, but they probably traveled farther, faster, and more profitably than any other car illustrated here. It is as if the Ford Trimotor aircraft, a contemporary of the Bullet car, were only now being taken out of first-line airline service.

The beetle-browed look of the Bullet car influenced many steam and diesel rail cars and locomotives, such as the Pullman 10000 and the Burlington Zephyr.

The true Art Deco interior is less austere than in later PCC types.

The bomber-like cockpit of the Bullet car was ahead of anything the Air Force had in 1931.

WASHINGTON, PRE-PCC, NUMBER 1053, 1935

SPECIFICATIONS	
LIVERY	CAPITAL TRANSIT CO.
TYPE	PRE-PCC
CAR NUMBER	1053
DATE	1935
BUILDER	ST. LOUIS CAR CO.
LENGTH	43FT. 7IN. (13.35M)
WEIGHT	34,750LB. (15,795KG)
SEATS	49
TRUCKS/WHEELS	DT

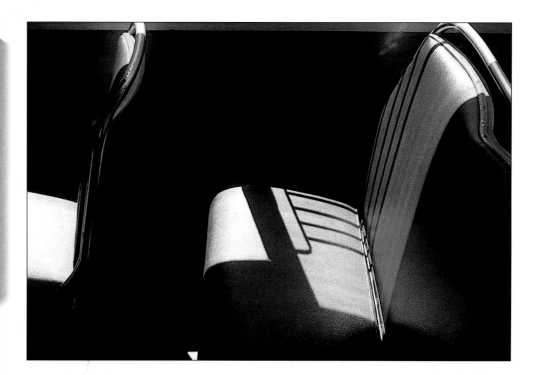

LEFT

The slick interior epitomized Art Deco functionality.

ABOVE

A sign at the rear step-well.

Even before the PCC design was finalized, the Capital Transit Co. had ordered some streamlined cars. These 20 cars, built by both J. G. Brill and the St. Louis Car Co. and delivered in 1935, had less refined running gear and boxier bodies than the 460 "true" PCC cars that ran in and around Washington, D.C., until 1962. Car number 1053, built by St. Louis Car Co. and the last survivor of the original 20, shows off the distinctive pressed metal stiffeners that resembled the "speedlines" then being applied to every object from toaster to skyscraper.

People took an immediate liking to the cars as they began service, and their appetites were whetted for the arrival of the much-vaunted PCCs two years later. In the green and gray livery of Capital Transit, and later DC Transit, they were as much a part of the scene as the Washington Monument. One of the drivers who drove PCC's along the Pennsylvania Avenue route remembers encountering then President Harry Truman a few times in the early 1950s, while the President was out for his legendary "morning constitutional," and, if he was lucky, catching a wave from the Chief Executive.

Of the 20 pioneer streamliners, only number 1053 was saved from the scrapman's torch when it was taken out of service at the close of the Eisenhower years in 1959.

Washington's first streamliner celebrates one more Cherry Blossom Festival at the National Capital Trolley Museum, just outside the city. The smooth, slab-sided exterior complements a smooth ride and acceleration. These cars were a hit with passengers from the very first.

BALTIMORE, PCC NUMBER 7407, 1944

SPECIFICATIONS	
LIVERY BALTIMORE TRANSIT CO.	
TYPE PCC	
CAR NUMBER 7407	
DATE 1944	
BUILDER PULLMAN	
LENGTH 46 FEET (14M)	
WEIGHT 37,900LB. (17,227KG)	
SEATS 54	
TRUCKS/WHEELS DT	

The PCC goes to war. Production priorities during World War II halted most assembly lines for cars, buses, and appliances, but trolleys, which consumed no scarce gasoline or rubber, regained a measure of importance in city transportation systems. Pullman kept its production lines open, and Baltimore bought number 7407 as one of its last streetcars in 1944. Shortages of raw materials meant that the chrome trim in the interiors had to be abandoned, paint being used instead, and some of the rubber inserts that gave PCC cars their quiet ride were omitted. Pullman simplified the exterior trim and eliminated a few compound curved metal panels for ease of manufacture, but these cars still gave sterling service for the duration of the war and long after. Number 7407 was the last PCC in service in the city, making its last run in 1963.

When you enter this PCC car today, it is disconcerting to see the bus-like driver's seat with accelerator and brake pedal and a petite speedometer, but no steering wheel, only a row of switches across the dashboard. The foot pedal replaced the old controller tower, resulting in much smoother acceleration. There were three discreet brake systems on the PCC – a regenerative brake, which fed stopping energy back into the power grid, a compressed air system, and an emergency magnetic system, which clamped down on the tracks. A 19-ton vehicle needed all the stopping power it could muster, especially in the fall, when wet leaves littered the tracks. The wetness wasn't a problem – it actually improved steel to steel friction – but the leaves were worse than sheet ice, as any veteran driver would attest.

OPPOSITE

The aggressive good looks of the PCC are set off by a prize-winning paint scheme, the result of a contest at the Maryland Institute.

ABOVE AND RIGHT

Single-ended PCCs came close to the perfect teardrop shape.

These pictures show the uncluttered ends of number 7407.

TORONTO, PCC NUMBER 4633, 1946

The typical bus-like looks of Toronto's PCCs. The streamlined styling seems to be in danger of getting in the way of visibility, even with additional "standee" windows in the red band at the top.

A close-up view shows the simple, tank-like construction, very unlike the more lightly built buses.

SPECIFICATIONS	
LIVERY	TORONTO TRANSIT
TYPE	PCC
CAR NUMBER	4633
DATE	1946
BUILDER	PULLMAN
LENGTH	46½ FEET (14.2M)
WEIGHT	40,000LB. (18,181KG)
SEATS	53
TRUCKS/WHEELS	DT

Toronto operated more PCCs by far than any other Canadian city. In all, 744 streamliners saw service between 1938 and the present, and in mid-1994 a few were still serving the city, as problems with proposed new LRV (light rail vehicle) systems continue.

Most of the earlier, prewar cars and those that were acquired secondhand were disposed of in 1983. The later, postwar examples, called all-electric because they exchanged air brakes for electric "fail-safe" brakes, can usually be distinguished by the additional row of "standee" windows running along the top of the car. Because of the rakish "chopped and dropped" windows on earlier PCCs, standing passengers could not see their stops. The new windows helped to overcome the problem,

allegedly being "lifted" from buses of the time. This was only fair, because buses had borrowed heavily from the PCC in their styling. Also of note in these newer PCC cars is the long dorsal pod containing ventilating fans, which, curiously, were never used by the Toronto Transportation Commission. The fans were removed, but the pods left in place. Brightly painted and un-numbered, car 4633, now out to pasture at the Halton County Radial Railway Museum, originally hails from Cleveland, Ohio. It is a Pullman-built all-electric car. Some machines were built for Toronto by the St. Louis Car Co. and by Canadian Car & Foundry, acting in partnership; others were originally built for Louisville, Kentucky. All were similar in size – slightly less than 47 feet (14.4m) long – and, of course, using the non-standard Toronto wide gauge of 4 feet 10⅞ inches (1.5m).

PHILADELPHIA, ELECTROLINER NUMBER 803, 804, 1941

SPECIFICATIONS

LIVERY
PHILADELPHIA

TYPE ELECTROLINER

CAR NUMBER 803, 804

DATE 1941

BUILDER
ST. LOUIS CAR CO.

LENGTH
156 FEET (47.5M)

WEIGHT
210,000LB. (95,455KG)

SEATS 141

TRUCKS/WHEELS DT

LEFT AND OPPOSITE

Greatly influenced by the revolutionary Burlington Zephyr of six years before, the train-like Electroliner has left the everyday trolley far behind.

ABOVE

A detail of the Zephyr-like roof headlight shows the influence of aviation, which was apparent everywhere in the 1930s.

As railroads began the transition from steam to diesel, they began introducing new engine designs called streamliners. Stealing a bit of thunder from these eye-catching models, the Electroliner was specifically designed to revitalize the bankrupt North Shore Line, which ran out of Chicago. The product of a three-year effort by the St. Louis Car Co. which began in 1938, the shovel-nosed speedster far exceeded expectations. Ridership on the line doubled in one year. Although the PCC cars had been out for only three years, the Electroliner's introduction in 1941 was a huge leap forward for interurban lines.

Among the amenities were true air conditioning, sound-proofing, and hydraulic shock absorbers. There was a luxurious bar where you could munch an Electroburger while cruising at 90mph (145kph) as the 1,000 horsepower of the Electroliner's eight motors whisked you toward Chicago's Loop.

Only two Electroliners were built, and when the North Shore Line gave them up in 1963, the Red Arrow Line of Philadelphia took them over. They ran in the same livery as the Bullet trains of 1931 until 1981, when the Rockhill Trolley Museum acquired one, shown here in its fading SEPTA colors.

CHAPTER FIVE

PARLOR CARS AND HEARSES

SPECIAL CARS

These cars, such as funeral cars, parlor cars, executive cars, and others developed for special needs, are fascinating to look over and are worth searching out.

Imagine having your own private railroad car, a sumptuously decorated home away from home, that, if you were the head of a regional railroad, you could use to tour your domain. Today's equivalent is the corporate business jet. Quite a few railroad magnates had rolling palaces like this, and the idea occurred to some trolley-line owners that they, too, should cruise their lines in a custom-built car. Probably the most famous of these special cars was the one built for H. E. Huntington of Pacific Electric. Built for speed as well as comfort, the "Alabama's" 800 horsepower could push the 55-ton 63-foot (19.2m) dreadnought to 90mph (145kph) and over. Inside and out, the car was the ultimate in 1905 luxury. Curved glass windshields and polished lacquer bodywork enclosed two staterooms, a dining room, and even a wood-burning fireplace.

Although the "Alabama" was in a class by itself, about 100 other parlor cars were built to varying standards of opulence throughout the U.S., although New England, in particular, and Massachusetts seem to have had more than their share. Most were eventually made available for charter use by the general public on special occasions. For $25 you would be whisked through town for a wedding reception or reunion dinner. Visiting politicians could see and be seen on mini-whistle-stop tours. Only six of these cars are known to survive today — even the "Alabama" met an undignified end in a kitchen fire. A look through the old photographs of the cars suggests that they were much alike. Most had all the requisites of Edwardian interior finery — red plush seats, dark oak or mahogany paneling, cut glass or art glass windows hung with velvet draperies, brass chandeliers, and even spittoons. There was just a hint of a high-class New Orleans bordello.

ABOVE

Interior detail of the Connecticut Traction Co. parlor car.

LEFT

The Atchison, Topeka postal car.

CONNECTICUT TRACTION CO., PARLOR
NUMBER 500, 1904

LEFT

Like the reclusive Miss Faversham in Great Expectations, the parlor car huddles in the back of the Shore Line Trolley Museum's barns. The yellow livery of the Connecticut Railway seems most inappropriate.

BELOW

Jules Verne-style instruments have an unstandardized, custom-built look that is typical of early electrical equipment.

Car number 500 is preserved in an almost unrestored state at the Shore Line Trolley Museum. Viewed in the darkened barn in Branford, Connecticut, there is little to hint of the car's appearance when new. Eliminate the garish yellow paint, remove the Pullman roof and enclosed platforms, restore the lace-like tracery of the open platform grillework, and it begins to look as it did in 1904. Inside, however, a time machine has brought us back 90 years and all is as it was: the oak carvings, wickerwork chairs, beveled mirrors, brass instruments, and even a rest room with stained glass windows. Dusty but intact, number 500 seems ready for diners to appear for a ghostly luncheon. It is hard to imagine that the Connecticut Traction Co. used its parlor car as recently as 1948.

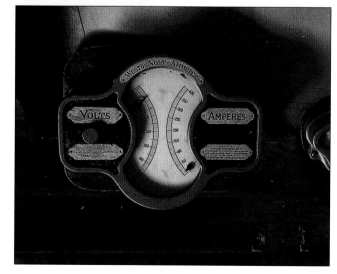

Old photographs show that absolutely nothing has changed since 1904. The stained glass doors leads to the restroom.

Some parlor cars could be rented for funerals. Other special cars were built specifically for this mordant task, and most cities had at least one funeral car. It had been the custom to have at least one of a city's trolley lines terminate at the cemetery, because there would be quite a lot of traffic on Sunday and holiday visits. Whether the trolley lines were being ghoulish and predatory or merely practical and providing a community service, the practice was adopted nearly world-wide. Durban, South Africa, had a couple of funeral cars, and Gothenburg, Sweden, had five. In Milan, cars ran on a dedicated line to the graveyard. In the U.S. some of the more extravagant cars were Baltimore's "Dolores" and "Lord Baltimore," and Providence, Rhode Island's "Oregon." Cleveland, Ohio, also had a car named "Dolores," which in Spanish can mean suffering. The car had a handsome, dark blue and gold livery with a gray oak interior and dark blue plush upholstery.

Other civic services performed by the nothing-if-not-versatile trolley ranged from the humdrum to the bizarre. There were postal trolleys in the U.S., Britain, and the Netherlands. Baltimore ran its last mail trolley in 1929. Montreal had a fleet of ominous black prison cars, from which, it is said, no one ever escaped. Munich had a library car. Some trolleys were used as ambulances, such as in Hanover in World War I, or as first-aid stations. In Minnesota, one "fire trolley" served for 23 years.

LOS ANGELES, FUNERAL CAR "DESCANSO", 1909

SPECIFICATIONS

LIVERY	LOS ANGELES RAILWAY
TYPE	FUNERAL CAR
CAR NUMBER	N/A
DATE	1909
BUILDER	LOS ANGELES RAILWAY
LENGTH	39FT. 2IN. (12M)
WEIGHT	35,000LB. (15,909KG)
SEATS	40
TRUCKS/WHEELS	DT

One of the finest hearse cars extant is named "Descanso," the Spanish for rest. Spanish names seem to be a recurring theme for these cars. "Descanso" has been preserved and restored at the Orange Empire Railway Museum. Built in 1909, this handsome gray and gold car carried funeral cortèges on the narrow-gauge Los Angeles Railway for many years before itself coming to rest high atop Cajon Pass in the California

LEFT

Many took their final trolley ride on this somber gray funeral car, which was built by the Los Angeles Railway.

OPPOSITE

Discreet gold striping spells out the name "Descanso."

ABOVE

The doors for sliding the coffin into the car were below the window.

RIGHT

Inside, dark wood arches and columns are very reminiscent of a chapel on wheels. The coffin would be placed below the door at the end of the car.

mountains, from where it was rescued in 1967. In its restored livery, "Descanso" appears ready for mourners to board. The immediate family went to the front of the car, where the coffin was in view, having been slid in discreetly from the side doors directly below the oval stained glass window. Other mourners traveled in a segregated rear compartment. All the fixtures are still in place for a tasteful and respectable trip to the cemetery. All this would be provided for a fee of around $25, which included formally uniformed driver and conductor.

ATCHISON, TOPEKA, POSTAL CAR NUMBER 60, 1924

SPECIFICATIONS

LIVERY	ATCHISON, TOPEKA
TYPE	MAIL CAR
CAR NUMBER	60
DATE	1924
BUILDER	P.C. & M.
LENGTH	64¼ FEET (19.6M)
WEIGHT	NOT KNOWN
SEATS	N/A
TRUCKS/WHEELS	DT

Keen-eyed readers will spot this car as an interloper in the book, for number 60 is a railroad coach and never ran as a trolley. But a photograph gives a hint of how similar cars, called RPOs, whether train or trolley, looked as they scuttled around town and countryside. As they ran, mail was sorted, often in windowless rooms. An illustration of a beautifully painted red, white, and blue post office car in *Popular Mechanics* magazine convinced one of the authors, then about five years old, that he should become a railroad postman. Perhaps fortunately, there were no more such jobs when he came of age.

RIGHT

This mail car has the look of an armored car. Note the trolley pole on roof for possible future operation at the Orange Empire Railway Museum at Perris.

CHAPTER SIX

MAINTAINING THE WAY

WORK CARS

Behind the scenes on every trolley line were cars used for maintenance – the grinders, line repair cars, snow sweepers, and so on. Their functional directness and often striking warning colors and graphic devices make them very photogenic.

These cars could hardly have been considered unobtrusive – 20 tons or more of metal and wood, with their 10-foot (3m) high, crudely boarded sides painted in glaring yellows and reds – but they worked behind the scenes to keep the revenue-producing trolleys running smoothly. They were little appreciated in their time and are today upstaged by the evocative and nostalgic passenger cars they once served. Although many of the cars described and illustrated in this book were rescued from forced service as work cars in their later years, at the turn of the century work cars were built from scratch. The catalogues of J. G. Brill and Stephenson were rife with snow-plows, sweepers, and sprinkler cars, not to mention baggage cars and freight handlers. Not only did traction companies have their own plant, track, and overhead wire to maintain, but in order to obtain easements and rights of way on public streets, most lines had to agree to maintain those streets. The companies undertook to keep them snow-free in winter and settle the dust in summer, and many built purpose-made cars in their own factories. These ranged from a few spare trucks and motors held together with a board platform on top, to line cars with extendible platforms that looked like medieval engines of war. They were called works or mains cars in Britain.

Later, as passenger trolleys were turned over to maintenance work, they found uses as paymaster's wagons and lunch cars, sand and salt carriers, or just mobile tool sheds. Few of these cars survived. They were even less likely to be preserved than their more comely sisters in revenue service. Those that have endured were more than likely left forgotten in some dark corner of a car barn.

ABOVE

Philadelphia freight car number 402.

LOS ANGELES, TOWER CAR NUMBER 9350, 1907

SPECIFICATIONS

LIVERY
LOS ANGELES

TYPE TOWER CAR

CAR NUMBER 9350

DATE 1907

BUILDER
LOS ANGELES RAILWAY

LENGTH
30FT. 4IN. (9.3M)

WEIGHT
38,600LB. (17,545KG)

SEATS N/A

TRUCKS/WHEELS DT

Very much a work in progress, the partially restored tower car, number 9350, motley paint job and all, exhibits a straightforward, no-nonsense design. Built in the Los Angeles Railway shops in 1907, a car like this can still do useful service, and the Orange Empire Railway Museum intends to get it back to work, tending the overhead lines, in return for a thorough spruce-up. The old wooden line cars can let men work safely even while trolley wires are live or "hot." The real disadvantage to a rig like this is that it cannot make way for other cars as it works, but this is a trivial problem at the museum.

ABOVE AND TOP

Paint and woodwork quickly fall victims to California's ferocious sun, as this close-up of the ladder (above) and the ratchet for the line platform mechanism (top) show.

PHILADELPHIA & WESTERN, SNOWPLOW

NUMBER 10, 1910

SPECIFICATIONS

LIVERY
PHILADELPHIA &
WESTERN

TYPE SNOWPLOW

CAR NUMBER 10

DATE 1910

BUILDER WASON

LENGTH
43 FEET (13.1M)

WEIGHT NOT KNOWN

SEATS N/A

TRUCKS/WHEELS DT

The winter of 1993 was a truly hard one, but it was just another working season to snowplow car number 10. This old campaigner has seen 84 winters. The people at the Rockhill Trolley Museum called it a lifesaver in this season of record-breaking snows, because it kept the tracks open and allowed them access to the sheds. Officially called a shear-type plow, cars like number 10 were designed to clear double track rights of way with the power of their four 75 horsepower motors. Old number 10, built by Wason in 1910, spent all its working life on the Philadelphia & Western line until acquisition by the museum in 1988. After restoration, the car looks like new in its dazzling yellow and black finish.

RIGHT

After the mighty blizzards of 1993, snowplow number 10 enjoys a deserved rest, basking in the Pennsylvania spring sun.

LOS ANGELES, WORK CRANE NUMBER 9225, 1912

This brawny machine still does useful work at the Orange Empire Railway Museum, as it has been doing since 1912. The Los Angeles Railway built number 9225 in its shops as a 40-foot (12.2m) long, five-ton derrick for tasks that could include placing derailed trolleys back on the tracks. It could still be seen intimidating drivers on the streets of Los Angeles in the mid-1950s.

ABOVE

A tramp freighter with its weathered hull and dangling gantries has the same scruffy look. The crane swivels through 360 degrees.

ABOVE AND RIGHT

The appearance of the headlight (above) is typical. A similar crane car in Connecticut (right) looks more purposeful and forbidding.

OPPOSITE

Even though number 9225 looks like a random collection of parts dumped on a flatbed, it can get the job done. The front cabin is the driver's cab.

O SHAWA, CANADA, WORK NUMBER W-28, 1917

Because some of Toronto's city track lines are still in use, the work cars here had long and varied careers. With the bright yellow paint of most of the other vehicles in non-revenue service, there is really nothing to distinguish number W-28 as a rail grinder. The grinding equipment is at track level and hidden inside the car. This job was one of the most important of the day-to-day maintenance tasks, ensuring passenger comfort and safety. Almost imperceptibly, especially at track joints, curves, and stops, undulations and irregularities build up in the hard, but malleable steel tracks, much like the "washboarding" seen on unpaved roads. To smooth these out, some grinders used revolving wheels; number W-28, however, used sliding abrasive blocks held to the tracks by air pressure.

Car number W-28 had been built as a passenger car in 1917, and it worked a snow scraper, numbered 2214, for a time until being rebuilt as a grinder. Retirement came in 1976. The museum has left it in work-car form, but its shedmate, number 55, was restored to its original configuration.

RIGHT

Enjoying a long-delayed retirement with a sparkling coat of yellow paint, number W-28 is probably cleaner now than it ever was as a work car. Just another trolley, it symbolizes the flexibility inherent in all these machines.

Toronto, Sweeper NUMBER S-37, 1920

SPECIFICATIONS

LIVERY
TORONTO TRANSIT

TYPE SNOW SWEEPER

CAR NUMBER S-37

DATE 1920

BUILDER RUSSELL

LENGTH
42½ FEET (12.9M)

WEIGHT
57,100LB. (25,955KG)

SEATS 4

TRUCKS/WHEELS DT

RIGHT

The well-worn bristles on these snow brushes are seen in detail, so low-tech they appear almost medieval, but they can still be found on street sweepers.

When there were only a few inches of snow, a rotating sweeper such as Toronto's number S-37 was perfect. As drifts mounted, plows such as number 10 (see page 109) were called out. Toronto bought a dozen of these large, double-truck cars from New York in 1947 to replace its aging, under-sized units. Number S-37 had originally been built for Boston, Massachusetts, in 1920, and they were not phased out until 1973, when the Halton County Radial Railway Museum acquired two of the cars.

PHILADELPHIA, FREIGHT NUMBER 402, 1920

There is a link, albeit tenuous, between this otherwise unremarkable work car and the Derby Locomotive of 1888 (see page 16). Car number 402 was built to haul freight, just as Van Depeole's machine was. For a time, the Eastern Michigan Railway System found it profitable to transport freight as a sideline, as did many Midwestern operators, although the steam railroads made it difficult for them by denying access to grade crossings and engaging in price wars, among other sharp practices. But places like Indianapolis grew into huge freight terminals and were able to guarantee same-day delivery within a radius of 75 miles (120km). A car like number 402 could actually pull standard railroad box cars as well as trolley freight trailers. As this cargo business declined with the rise of long-haul trucking, number 402 was sold, in 1943, to Philadelphia & Western as a line car, and it bears that company's partially restored colors.

Nowadays this wheeled box seems about as far away from the picturesque world of streetcars as you can get, but freight trolleys like this once gave steam railroad owners ulcers.

What a concept! A self-powered freight car seems unbeatable, but would you really want these monsters cruising around your town's streets?

OTTAWA, LINE NUMBER 25, 1923

SPECIFICATIONS

LIVERY
OTTAWA ELECTRIC
RAILWAY

TYPE MAINTENANCE

CAR NUMBER 25

DATE 1923

BUILDER
OTTAWA ELECTRIC
RAILWAY

LENGTH
30 FEET (9.1M)

WEIGHT
23,000LB. (10,455KG)

SEATS N/A

TRUCKS/WHEELS ST

Ignore, if you can, the bright new caboose-red paintwork, and instead concentrate on the wooden framework unobtrusively mounted on the side of car number 25. This tower can be extended to twice the height of the car, and the platform can be rotated to allow access to any part of the overhead power lines or their supporting guy wires. Ottawa Electric Railway's own workshops produced this single-truck workhorse in 1923.

ABOVE

The newly restored paintwork demonstrates the attention-getting qualities of fire engine red number 25.

LEFT AND OPPOSITE

The framework extended to about 12 feet (3.7m) and the platform at the top pivoted. The non-conductive wooden structure guarded against shock, so lines could be serviced while they were still live.

CHAPTER SEVEN

LIVERIES OF THE WORLD

In this final chapter we look at the colors, signs, logos, and other graphic devices used throughout the world to show destinations and fares and to advertise products on trolley cars throughout their early history. A trolley's number was its name and usually stayed with it forever, just as with locomotives.

Trolleys were a colorful breed, a legacy of their horsecar antecedents. In an era of great civic pride and fascination with all things mechanical, was it any wonder that the early cars were tricked out in bright, eye-catching colors? It was not just a question of practicality and the need to identify one car route from another. If someone had built a trolley line, he was proud of it and wanted his name in clearly visible letters. If Johnstown, Pennsylvania, was putting in a streetcar system, the whole town should know that the livery was orange-yellow and white. In the early years, colors, shapes, and letterforms blended in with the townscape, and attempts were made, in the U.S. at least, to make sure that the architecture of buildings and vehicles were of a piece.

A 19th-century tradition of "beautifying" machinery with applied decoration continued for a surprisingly long time with trolleys – much later than for the typical automobile or steam railroad carriage – especially on exterior surfaces. Most trolleys were given a two-color scheme, with elaborate striping defining panel lines in contrasting colors, or in gold or silver leaf. Lettering usually had complex outlining and shadowing. The running gear, trucks, chassis, and the like sometimes also received this treatment, but usually they were left in a subdued single color such as black or red oxide. That this theme occurred consistently in every industrialized nation says much about the prevalence of Edwardian style and sensibility.

As time went on, European trams seemed to lean more toward often bright, single-color schemes. It was an almost universal practice to apply ancient city coats of arms and crests to municipally owned vehicles. In Britain, the colors were usually

more subdued, but, together with city crests or devices, came advertising panels, particularly on the upper decks of the city cars. American cars, which had pioneered the use of internal advertising cards in the horsecar era, inexplicably resisted the urge to plaster advertisements on the sides of trolleys, except for temporary, usually company-related, announcements of football games, picnics, and so forth. Perhaps a tenuous link with the dignified and unadorned railroads kept the trolley lines pristine.

Later, two trends emerged in North America: in the city, trolleys began to be a little more strident in their colors, with yellows and oranges predominating. The interurban lines, on

Car number 629, 3rd Avenue Railway Co., New York. The large letter at the lower left gave each route a letter code: T for Tremont Ave, X for Crosstown.

Public Service, Jersey City.

Servico de Transportes Colectivos do Porto, Portugal.

Johnstown Traction Co., Pennsylvania.

Vienna, Austria.

Toronto Transportation, Canada.

Graz, Austria.

Great Northern Railway, Ireland.

San Francisco Municipal Railway, California.

Car number 316, Union Railway, New York. The lighted route box looks like an afterthought.

the other hand, followed the lead of the steam railroads once again, with Pullman green the favorite, perhaps in the hope that the cachet of the sober establishment colors would rub off on the upstart interurbans. The Chicago line was dark green and red, and a lighter shade of green was used by Cleveland Southwestern, which was dubbed the Green Line. An exception to the rule were the extroverted "Big Red" cars of Pacific Electric, and other interurbans used red for their specially named lines such as the Red Arrow Line and the Red Devil Special.

Not all trolley lines went to garish extremes. When the PCC cars arrived in Baltimore, they were considered so handsome that a competition was held at the Maryland Institute to come

up with a worthy color scheme. As illustrated by the Baltimore Museum's number 7407 (see page 92), a most fitting choice was made: Alexandria blue and light gray, with an orange "cheat line." When war preparations galvanized the U.S. in 1942, Civil Defense officials decided that Baltimore's PCCs must be camouflaged, and fawn was substituted for gray on the cars' rooftops. Whether this was effective against the city's red brick streets is open to doubt, but one old-timer told us, "At least it showed we were doing our part."

The exigencies of war in Britain led to several British trams being painted gray or olive drab, and some had white bumpers so that they were visible during blackouts. Numerous German trams received full camouflage coats of tan, with green and brown dappling.

During the 1930s, as PCCs and streamliners took over, especially in the U.S., stripes and scallops were reintroduced, but this time their inspiration seemed to be flashy paint schemes flaunted by racing aircraft such as the "Gee Bee" and other teardrop-shaped craft. These were banners of an optimistic era. Still later, with the decline of the trolley and the fading of once-proud liveries, utilitarian, single-color schemes of creamy or dull-colored yellow and the hateful "traction orange" were the rule.

When the early sparkers first began to ply their routes, some using the old cable car right of way, there were so few of them that little thought was given to route indicators. Most cars were assigned to only one route all their working lives, so all pertinent information was painted on the car. Sometimes colored glass clerestories would be used. The ruby glass

Car number 264, Baltimore, Maryland. The etched glass ends of clerestory would glow at night.

Car number 2001, Montreal, Canada. A back view of the Hunter-type destination blinds that could be rolled to change numbers.

Car number 356, Johnstown, Pennsylvania. Another rolling destination blind in a side window of a Birney Safety Car.

Derby Loco, Connecticut. The full name of the line always appeared on the sides of early cars.

Car number 1164, Baltimore, Maryland. The semipermanent letter board showed the destinations in a vestige of horse-car days.

Red Arrow logo, Rockhill.

clerestory windows of Providence car number 61, while looking stylish, served also to denote the route, especially at night, as did the red and cream paintwork, and it matched the purple, orange, and green glass in the fellow cars on other routes throughout the city. In Britain, some routes in Scotland used variations in upper deck colors to denote routes. Still others solved the problem for night service with patterns of colored lights. Edinburgh and Toronto used this method.

As new routes and lines proliferated, passenger confusion grew apace, and so a host of devices arose for indicating route number and direction, some primitive and some ingenious, to help the poor traveler get home. The simplest were removable panels which clipped onto the dashboard or roof and showed route numbers or destinations. Sometimes, as in Plymouth, England, these were in color, but usually they were stark black and white. Changeable cut-out metal stencils with backlighting were common for a while, until the patented system of fabric roller blinds we all know became standard.

Taylor truck logo. Branford Castings often carried prominent patent numbers.

Japanese truck logo, Rockhill. A curious narrow-gauge replacement truck.

Car numbers.

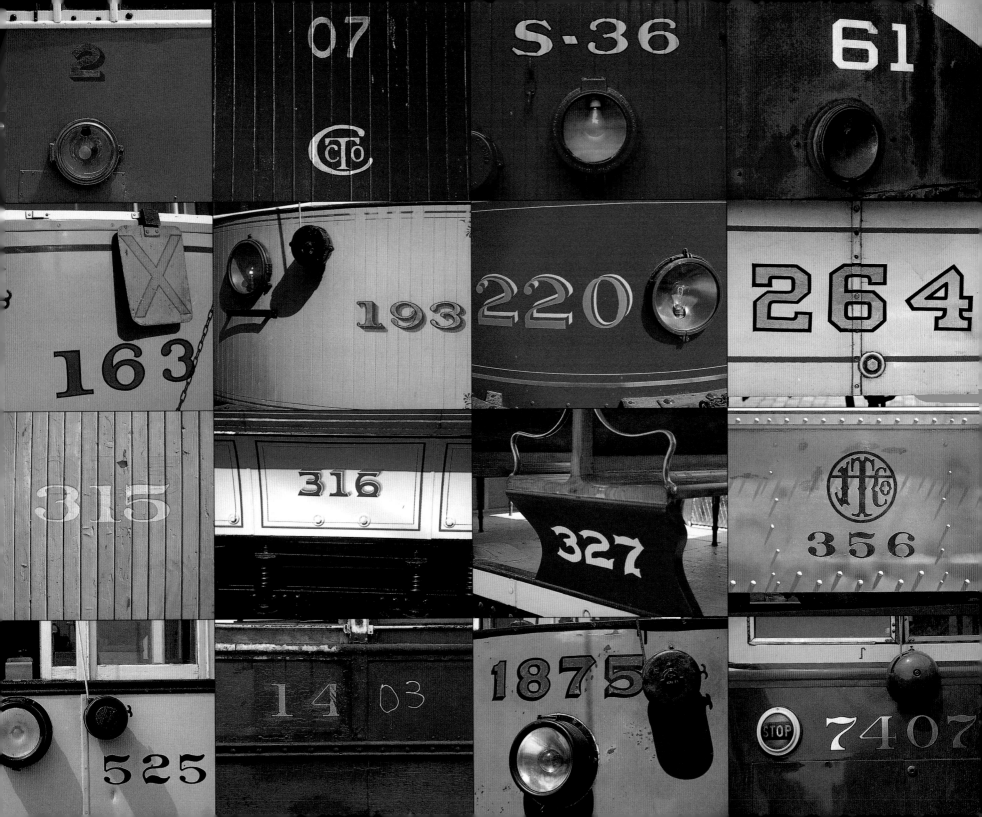

MUSEUMS TO VISIT

This is only a partial listing of the major museums and collections around the world. All the trolleys and trams illustrated in this book can be seen at these locations, and in most cases excursion rides are offered on short, scenic stretches of track to give trips back to the time when trolley travel brought the city to the country. There are many other fine collections of preserved trams and streetcars all over the world.

U.S.A.

Shore Line Trolley Museum
17 River Street
East Haven CT 06512
(203) 467 – 6927

Rockhill Trolley Museum
Railways to Yesterday, Inc.
PO Box 1601
Allentown PA 18105
(814) 447 – 9576

National Capital Trolley Museum
PO Box 4007
Silver Spring MD 20914
(301) 384 – 6352

Baltimore Streetcar Museum
PO Box 4881
Baltimore MD 21211
(301) 547 0264

Orange Empire Railway Museum
PO Box 548
Perris CA 92572-0548
(909) 657 – 2605

Halton County Radial Railway Museum
R.R. #2
Rockwood, Ontario
N0B 2K0

U.K.

National Tramway Museum
Crich
Matlock
Derbyshire

London Transport Museum
49 The Piazza
Covent Garden
London WC2

Glasgow Museum of Transport
Kelvin Hall
1 Bunhouse Road
Glasgow G3 8DP

AUSTRIA

Graz Tramway Museum
Keplerstrasse 105
8021 Graz

FRANCE

Fédération des Amis des Chemins de Fer Secondaires
134 rue de Rennes
75006 Paris
Musée des Transports-Urbain
60 avenue Sainte-Marie
94160 Saint-Mandé

ITALY

Museo Dei Transporti Italian
Via Alberto 99
21020 Ranco

ACKNOWLEDGMENTS

Thanks to all the staff members of all the museums who helped us get these photos. This includes: The Halton County Museum, The Shore Line Museum, especially George Boucher and Ron Parente, The National Capitol Museum especially Ken Rucker and Ham Sissum, The Baltimore Streetcar Museum with particular thanks to Andy Blumberg and Dan Lawrence, The Orange County Museum, especially Paul Hammond and Wally Richards, The Rockhill Museum especially Joel and Carl Salomon. Thanks also to Glynn Wilton of the Crich Museum for some critical help, and thanks to the members of the Electric Railroaders' Association in New York, especially Frank Miklos, Ken Oskosciewicz and Dennis Linsky. Help from the staff of both the Midtown Branch and the Main Branch of the New York Public Library and from the staff of the Red Caboose in New York is also appreciated. Thank you also to The London Transport Museum, Covent Garden and all those museums who responded to our inquiries but whom we did not get to visit. Also thanks go to Barbara Shelley, Jon Lopez, Susan DiBarba, Muriel Mentze, and Stu Leitener for all their help and encouragement, and the people at Quintet, including Helen Denholm and Steven Paul.

INDEX